Autism Working

by the same authors

Having Fun with Feelings on the Autism Spectrum
A CBT Activity Book for Kids Age 4–8
Michelle Garnett, Tony Attwood, Louise Ford, Stefanie Runham and Julia Cook
ISBN 978 1 78775 327 3
eISBN 978 1 78775 328 0

10 Steps to Reducing Your Child's Anxiety on the Autism Spectrum
The CBT-Based 'Fun with Feelings' Parent Manual
Michelle Garnett, Tony Attwood, Louise Ford, Stefanie Runham and Julia Cook
ISBN 978 1 78775 325 9
eISBN 978 1 78775 326 6

Exploring Depression, and Beating the Blues
A CBT Self-Help Guide to Understanding and Coping with
Depression in Asperger's Syndrome [ASD-Level 1]
Tony Attwood and Michelle Garnett
Illustrated by Colin Thompson
ISBN 978 1 84905 502 4
eISBN 978 0 85700 907 4

CBT to Help Young People with Asperger's Syndrome (Autism
Spectrum Disorder) to Understand and Express Affection
A Manual for Professionals
Tony Attwood and Michelle Garnett
ISBN 978 1 84905 412 6
eISBN 978 0 85700 801 5

From Like to Love for Young People with Asperger's
Syndrome (Autism Spectrum Disorder)
Learning How to Express and Enjoy Affection with Family and Friends
Tony Attwood and Michelle Garnett
ISBN 978 1 84905 436 2
eISBN 978 0 85700 777 3

AUTISM WORKING

A Seven-Stage Plan to Thriving at Work

Michelle Garnett and Tony Attwood

Jessica Kingsley Publishers
London and Philadelphia

First published in Great Britain in 2022 by Jessica Kingsley Publishers
An Hachette Company

4

Copyright © Michelle Garnett and Tony Attwood 2022

The right of Michelle Garnett and Tony Attwood to be identified as
the Authors of the Work has been asserted by them in accordance
with the Copyright, Designs and Patents Act 1988.

Front cover image source: Shutterstock®.

A CIP catalogue record for this title is available from the
British Library and the Library of Congress

ISBN 978 1 78775 983 1
eISBN 978 1 78775 984 8

Printed and bound in Great Britain by CPI Group (UK) Ltd, Croydon CR0 4YY

Jessica Kingsley Publishers' policy is to use papers that are natural, renewable
and recyclable products and made from wood grown in sustainable
forests. The logging and manufacturing processes are expected to
conform to the environmental regulations of the country of origin.

Jessica Kingsley Publishers
Carmelite House
50 Victoria Embankment
London EC4Y 0DZ

www.jkp.com

Contents

Preface

Getting and keeping a job is not easy for someone who has autism. A recent survey indicated that over 73 per cent of autistic adults have concerns about getting and keeping a job (Attwood, Evans and Lesko 2014). An online research survey of over 400 autistic adults found that only 24 per cent were employed full time and 16 per cent part time. The study also found that in comparison to neurotypical (non-autistic) respondents, those with autism were statistically more likely to have been signed off from work for at least two months due to anxiety, depression or another mental health reason, spent at least a year unemployed and seeking work, had disciplinary action taken against them or been sacked, or left a job because of being badly treated by colleagues (Griffiths *et al.* 2019). Parents also have their concerns, and they consider employment support as their greatest service priority (Neary, Gilmore and Ashburner 2015). We also know that having a university degree does not automatically lead to employment success, with few autistic adults working in their undergraduate field of study (Loundes-Taylor, Henninger and Mailick 2015). When we consider those with autism who have a job, many are under-employed, that is, their job does not match the person's abilities, qualifications and aspirations (Griffiths *et al.* 2019).

This is despite autism being associated with qualities that are sought by employers such as reliability, accuracy, persistence, attention to detail, liking routines and procedures, creativity in problem-solving, extensive factual and technical knowledge, a strong sense of social justice, not letting socializing be a distraction, being talented in identifying errors for quality control and a natural ability with cataloguing information and identifying patterns and sequences.

Having a successful career will significantly improve self-worth and self-identity, provide structure and purpose to the day, an opportunity to make friends, increase income and greater financial independence, and be an effective antidote to low self-esteem and depression.

Autism Working was written to assist readers to understand how the characteristics of autism will affect employment, and to provide strategies to accommodate those characteristics in a work environment. Thus, the book will be valuable for those who are employed, but can also be valuable as a programme in preparation for future employment or a change in employment.

From our extensive clinical experience we consider that no job or career would automatically be viewed as impossible due to having autism. This can include the expected careers in engineering, information technology, accounting and being a scientist at university, but also a career in the arts in terms of being a fine artist, musician or author. We have also known autistic adults who have been successful in the caring professions, from nursing to psychology, as well as the military, police force and politics, and careers caring for animals such as being a vet or zookeeper. There is no automatic restriction on choice of career if someone has autism.

How to choose that career? The first option may be to see if there are employment prospects related to a special interest or talent that is associated with the person's profile of autism and personality. A childhood special interest in LEGO® that develops during adolescence into an intense interest in the design of machines could become the basis of a successful career in mechanical engineering. A fascination with friendship in childhood may develop into an interest in psychology in adolescence, and success in a caring profession, for example, as a counsellor or clinical psychologist in adulthood.

We highly recommend that autistic adolescents have a detailed assessment of vocational abilities during their secondary school years to identify whether a special interest could be the foundation of a potential career and an assessment identifying areas of vocational abilities for improvement. This information should then be included in the secondary school curriculum. When there is a history of failed employment experiences, this can provide valuable information on what skills or employment accommodations are needed and which jobs or workplaces to avoid. It may take several employment experiences before finding the right job with the right employer.

When searching for a job that matches abilities, interests, qualifications and personality, it is important to find as much information as possible on the social and sensory aspects of the job and, if feasible, the attitude of the line manager and workmates or colleagues to someone who has the characteristics of autism. Autistic people can sometimes have a 'sixth sense' to quickly appraise the social atmosphere of a new situation, and a positive or negative attitude can become apparent on meeting the staff and seeing the work environment prior to or during the interview process. We recommend trusting that intuition.

There will probably be a need for guidance in completing the application form and in particular, deciding whether to disclose the diagnosis. There are no clear rules on disclosure when applying for a job, and it is sometimes a personal decision based on whether disclosure would facilitate or inhibit achieving an interview. It is also important to decide what to wear for the interview and to rehearse how to answer the anticipated questions during the interview. If autism has been disclosed in the application, it may be an advantage to prepare a brief brochure on autism and associated qualities in relation to the position. The brochure can be attached to the application or given to those conducting the interview.

A job interview is a complex social ordeal. There is an expectation of accurately reading the body language of those conducting the interview, and succinctly and honestly answering their questions. A candidate who has autism may have difficulty knowing the non-verbal signals and social conventions in an interview. We highly recommend practice and rehearsal in interviewing techniques, and having an informative portfolio of relevant work experience that can be the focus of the interaction. If those conducting the interview know that the person has autism, it will help to be honest and describe some of the difficulties associated with autism, but that these are significantly less than the qualities associated with autism for the position, and that there are strategies to facilitate successful employment. This book was written to provide those strategies.

In previous generations, autistic men were most likely to have a career as craftsmen such as watch makers, jewellers and carpenters. These could be solitary pursuits with an emphasis on quality rather than quantity, with relatively little stress compared to modern society with an emphasis on production rates and social networking. Historically, women had fewer career opportunities and were actively discouraged from joining the workforce as well as some careers, including medicine, law and the church. Whilst modern work practices and expectations have opened the path for autistic men and women to join the workplace across all fields of endeavour, modern workplaces cause great stress and distress for those who have autism.

Any career or specific employment position must be evaluated in terms of stress levels and coping with changes in the job requirements, workload and the social and interpersonal dynamics of the job. *Autism Working* was designed to provide an autistic employee with specific strategies to cope with stress, any sensory processing differences, social communication issues and executive functioning difficulties at work. Armed with these strategies, a successful career is within reach for the autistic employee.

Introduction

Purpose of the *Autism Working* programme

Welcome to *Autism Working*. This programme has been designed to assist people with an autism spectrum disorder (ASD) level 1 (formerly known as Asperger's syndrome) to become ready for employment and to achieve success and progress in their workplace.

We hold the following principles to be true, and these underpin the entire programme:

> People on the autism spectrum bring many gifts and strengths to the community, including their workplace. They experience a different, not defective, way of perceiving, thinking, learning and relating. This profile of abilities can contribute to a successful career. However, they will require a work culture that is supportive, open-minded, flexible, respectful and knowledgeable of the characteristics of autism.

The programme is designed as a self-help manual that is home-based. The advantage of a home-based programme is that the activities for each stage of the programme can be conducted with maximum motivation, attention and clarity of thought. The activities and stages can be dispersed throughout the day or week. The amount of time to complete a specific activity can be extended, if needed, with a greater opportunity for reflection, exploration of examples and practical application in a work environment. However, it is also important to recognize and accommodate the problems associated with a home-based programme, such as distractions (the television or computer as well as domestic or family chores).

Please note that all the written material you need is in this book, including the questionnaires and activities. To access all the audio and video recordings, as well as the soft copy of the Personal Employment Plan, go to the JKP Library at https://library.jkp.com/redeem and use the voucher code MMWZXGG

Programme materials and description

The *Autism Working* programme was originally designed to be delivered over seven stages, each two hours long, with a small group of adults who have autism and who are seeking employment or who need advice to maintain their employment and achieve promotion within the workplace. We encourage you to work through each stage at your own pace, dedicating two hours per week to each stage, if you can. Each stage represents a tool in the *Autism Working Toolbox*. The 'toolbox' analogy is one we have found to be highly successful in equipping autistic people to embrace their strengths and manage their challenges. Stages 1–6 in the programme correspond to six important sets of Tools in the Toolbox:

1. Stress Management Tools
2. Sensory Management Tools
3. Social Tools
4. Awareness Tools
5. Thinking Tools
6. Organizational Tools.

These six stages were carefully chosen and designed to directly address key problems that can occur in the workplace for an autistic person, based on research and our clinical experience.

The seventh stage is designed to incorporate and consolidate previous learning through the introduction of the *Personal Employment Plan*. You will spend this stage creating a Personal Employment Plan, incorporating not only previously learned material, but also personal goal setting, planning, setting up your support team and a self-monitoring plan. The Personal Employment Plan is designed to be both a planning and a communication tool.

This programme is designed so that your most important areas for growth can be identified, assessed, and a plan made to address the problems identified. Using specifically designed questionnaires that you complete during the course, the most important strengths and challenges for you are identified. Also included in the course are eight videos explaining aspects of autism relevant to the workplace.

The course includes personal reflection, completing activities and consultation with a mentor. These learning modalities will provide you with ideas and strategies to address any problems that may be occurring either in the work or home setting that are current or potential barriers to your success at work.

We encourage you to choose your own area/s for growth, based on your own learning through the programme. Completing the programme will give you a range of tools that you need to set and achieve your employment goals. Your Personal Employment Plan can be shared with your support team who can then meaningfully assist you in meeting your goals. The Personal Employment Plan may be downloaded in soft copy format to allow you to use the format over and over again, as both a planning and a communication tool within your work setting.

Programme materials

- Eight video recordings
- Six questionnaires
- Activities for each of the six stages
- Personal Employment Plan
- Two audio recordings
- Three video recordings to explain the course to your support team.

List of video recordings

- 1.1 The interplay between stress and autism
- 1.2 Learning to relax
- 2. Sensory perception and autism
- 3. Social difficulties and autism
- 4. Meditation resources

- 5. Recognizing and challenging your own thinking patterns
- 6.1 Thinking and learning abilities in autism
- 6.2 Strategies for organizational difficulties.

List of questionnaires

- 1.1 Strengths and Challenges within the Workplace
- 1.2 Signs of Anxiety and Stress Scale
- 1.3 What Makes You Stressed?
- 1.4 Depression, Anxiety and Stress Scale-21 (DASS-21)
- 2.1 Sensory Perception
- 6.1 Thinking and Learning Talents
- 6.2 Cognitive or Organizational Difficulties.

List of video recordings for a support team

- What is autism?
- How do I work productively with an autistic person in the workplace?
- Social communication and autism in the workplace.

List of audio recordings

- Progressive muscle relaxation
- Meditation.

An additional resource

The Depression, Anxiety and Stress Scale-21 (DASS-21) is not part of the *Autism Working* set of materials, and so is not in your pre-course questionnaire pack, *but it will be needed during the programme, and is readily available for free online.*[1] Complete and score this questionnaire prior to commencing the programme.

---

1   You can either go to www2.psy.unsw.edu.au/dass or type 'Depression Anxiety and Stress Scales' into your search engine.

Guidance from a mentor

The *Autism Working* programme is a self-help intervention. However, research indicates that the most efficient and effective way to incorporate a self-help intervention is to follow the programme under guidance from a mentor. We therefore *highly recommend* that you have a mentor who can be consulted to assist with self-understanding, providing an alternative perspective and a wider range of strategies. The mentor may be a family member, support person, perhaps someone from an employment agency, friend, life coach or clinical psychologist.

Support may be given via face-to-face conversation, the internet, telephone, email, or any other communication method that you prefer.

Whilst we highly recommend that you undertake the programme with the assistance of a mentor, we understand that this may not be either a possible or desirable option for you. In this case, it is entirely possible to complete the programme as a self-directed solitary endeavour.

Whether you choose to complete the programme in a self-directed way or with the guidance of a mentor, it will be important for you or your mentor to become aware of your own personal learning style. Adapting and accommodating your own learning style will enhance the effectiveness of the *Autism Working* programme.

Unique learning style within autism

Your unique learning style is why you will be highly employable, but it could also provide some challenges in the workplace. Autistic people have atypical perception, learning and thinking styles, which include learning talents, but also learning difficulties. This section has been included to assist you to recognize, understand and accommodate your own distinct learning style.

A need for consistency and certainty

Autistic people seem to have a strong desire to seek consistency and certainty in their daily lives. They thrive on routine and predictability. They also often need careful mental preparation for unexpected change and at times of transition. When working through this programme, whether by yourself or with a mentor, we recommend setting aside a specific time slot, every week or every two to three days for the activities, depending on how quickly you wish to complete the course. Ensure that the time span chosen suits your concentration span, up to 50 minutes at a time. Place these time slots in your diary and honour them as if they were particularly important meetings, for example, a job interview or a meeting with your employer. This technique will not only provide predictability, but will also ensure the consistent commitment needed in the programme to bring about the positive changes that will encourage successful career outcomes.

Intellectual strengths in learning

It is common in autism for someone to have a considerable difference between their visual and verbal thinking abilities and learning style. For example, you may have stronger visual thinking skills than verbal skills – you learn more by watching than listening. In this case, you will greatly benefit from the learning available in the video recordings, visualizing yourself using the new skills, as well as role-plays with your mentor.

If you have stronger verbal than visual skills, you will highly value and learn most from pre-reading texts, discussions with your mentor and from writing down and re-reading your self-reflections.

Regardless of learning style, you will benefit from real-life practice of the skills and self-reflection on your learning afterwards.

ACCOMMODATING DIFFERENT LEARNING STYLES

- Know your own learning style (visual or verbal), and share this with your mentor.
- Throughout the stages of the programme be sure to use both visual (role-play, demonstration, practical exercises, visualization) and verbal (reading, writing, discussion) modalities.

Attentional difficulties

Autistic people often have attentional difficulties, including being able to sustain attention for long periods on topics when they are not interested or are confused, paying prolonged attention to relevant information, shifting attention to new topics and distractibility, including being distracted by their inner imagination (for example, day dreaming) and sensory experiences. In addition, some autistic people may be impulsive and overactive with motor restlessness (difficulty sitting still).

ACCOMMODATING ATTENTIONAL DIFFICULTIES

- 'Chunk' the material you must concentrate on into discrete activities, so that each activity doesn't take longer than 10–20 minutes followed by a mental break.
- Use a mental break to help you transition to the next activity. For example, after completing a reading, watching or writing activity, say to yourself: 'Okay, that is the end of that activity.' Stand up and take a movement break before you start the next activity.
- You may benefit from a support person to assist you to stay on track with the programme materials.
- Use a highlighter pen to identify key information within the activities. This will make it easier to come back and identify what you most need from that stage.
- Work on the activities in a setting that has few, if any, distractions and aversive sensory experiences.
- Schedule regular breaks and rotate between types of activity to enhance your attention and learning capacity.

Problems with organizational and planning skills

Many autistic people also have a diagnosis of attention deficit disorder (ADD) or attention deficit hyperactivity disorder (ADHD), or fragments of these conditions; hence you may know that you have some problems in the areas of what is described as 'executive functioning', which includes organizational and planning skills, time management, planning, multitasking, working memory (in particular, memory for spoken instructions), procrastination and priorities.

ACCOMMODATING PROBLEMS WITH ORGANIZATIONAL AND PLANNING SKILLS

- Ensure all electronic devices are switched off and put away for the duration of the stage.
- Allow for two short (2–3 minutes) and one long (15 minute) break between each activity in each stage.
- Work on the programme in a quiet room with minimal visual and auditory distractions and a comfortable seat each time.
- Use sensory or fidget toys to assist with attention, or perhaps play calming music in the background.
- There are reading, listening, reflective, interactive and writing or typing activities. It is helpful to only do one of these activities at any one time.

The programme rotates between a variety of activities, including reading, writing, reflecting, watching videos, practice exercises and discussions with your mentor, if you have opted to have one. This is designed to keep concentration and energy levels high. However, if your energy flags, we recommend having some new activities prepared, such as:

- A relaxing yoga pose, for example, downward dog, feet up the wall or child's pose
- Take a stretch and a walk around the room or outdoors. Make a cup of tea or coffee
- A 3-minute mindfulness activity; for example, focus your attention on the information coming into your awareness through each of the five senses, one at a time, with your eyes closed.

A one-track mind

If you have autism it can be difficult to consider an alternative perspective or strategy. This rigidity in thinking style may be termed having a 'one-track mind', where the person seems restricted to one strategy and has difficulty being flexible in thinking and incorporating new information or trying something new. Having a one-track mind is very common in autism. However, we have found that this rigidity is lessened when the person is more confident and relaxed. Thus, this thinking style can become more of a problem during times of high anxiety or stress.

ACCOMMODATING PROBLEMS WITH A ONE-TRACK MIND

- Relax and consider several perspectives and strategies. Give yourself a compliment for creating each perspective or strategy; for example, 'Well done, that is a great idea.'
- Take some time to engage in a completely different activity that engages another part of the brain before you need to be flexible in your thinking; for example, go for a walk or engage in a 3-minute self-awareness activity, as described later.
- Write down your ideas, regardless of how ridiculous or useless they may seem, as they are being formed in your mind. Be open. Many people on the autism spectrum describe that they have their best ideas when they can be free to self-express, with no judgement.
- If you are very tense or stressed about a problem, use the audio recording 'Progressive muscle relaxation' to give your body a break from the tension, or use the Thinking Tools described in Stage 5, especially the 'unhelpful thinking styles' section, to assist you to manage any unhelpful and/or unrealistic or negative thought patterns that are getting in the way.
- Have a discussion with your mentor for any other ways of encouraging flexible thinking.

Fear of making a mistake

Autistic people are very prone to having a fear of making a mistake, or performance anxiety. A characteristic of autism is a determination to be perceived by others as being intelligent. Unfortunately, making a mistake may lead to a misperception of being incompetent or stupid. There can also be a fear of being judged or ridiculed by others. You may experience extreme emotional distress in the face of possibly making a mistake, or the potential of having a failure experience or of being evaluated.

ACCOMMODATING PROBLEMS WITH FEAR OF MAKING A MISTAKE

- Praise and encourage yourself for any suggestion or answer you write down.

- Adopt a positive problem-solving approach, reminding yourself that 'mistakes' are an important part of the learning process, assisting us to learn. Making a mistake does not mean you are stupid.
- Remember that if you become anxious about making a mistake, your thinking will be less flexible and rational. If you stay calm, you will be smarter.

Special interests

Many autistic people develop many special interests throughout their lives. These can be a source of self-esteem, a means of making friends with others who share the same interest, a thought blocker for anxiety, an energizer when exhausted or feeling depressed, and potentially, the basis for a successful and rewarding career path due to recognized abilities developed through the amount of time enjoying the special interest.

The interest may be used within the *Autism Working* programme to increase your engagement, understanding of concepts and memory. For example, one of our group participants, an early childhood teacher, had a special interest and talent in education. She used her talent as an educator to summarize the material in the *Autism Working* programme using colourful visuals and colour coding, which helped her not only remember and conceptualize the material, but also to use the material later within her working life.

ACCOMMODATING SPECIAL INTERESTS

- Write down your special interest(s) and all the abilities and talents you have acquired and use to engage in your interest:

  _____

  _____

  _____

  _____

  _____

- Use your special interest(s) as a point of reference or metaphor throughout the programme if you become stuck with understanding a concept or knowing what to do. For example, if your interest is Dr Who, remind yourself that Dr Who is always calm and rational in a crisis.

Alexithymia

Approximately 80 per cent of autistic people experience alexithymia, which is a condition where the person has a limited vocabulary to describe their emotional experiences or feelings through speech. The person may be able to describe basic feelings, such as happy and sad, but can struggle to describe more subtle or complex emotions, for example, feeling mildly irritated, confused, jealous or embarrassed. It is important to be aware that if you do not easily have the words to describe your feelings or thoughts, there may need to be accommodations to assist you at work.

ACCOMMODATING PROBLEMS WITH ALEXITHYMIA

- Should the precise word to accurately describe your feelings be elusive, you could quantify the degree of expression using a thermometer or numerical rating, perhaps from 0 to 100, thus indicating the perceived intensity of emotional experience.
- Use a different mode of communication, for example, saying that your feelings are described eloquently by a specific song or piece of music, or looking for images or pictures from the internet, as 'a picture is worth a thousand words'.
- Type an email explaining your thoughts and feelings. Sometimes it is easier to type your thoughts and feelings rather than explain them during a conversation.
- Try to explain your thoughts and feelings to your mentor for their advice or record them on camera, and watch the video to see whether what you said matches your thoughts and feelings.

Difficulty with self-disclosure at work

Not only can an autistic person frequently experience difficulty expressing their feelings due to alexithymia, they can also experience considerable difficulty with questions such as, 'Why did you do that?', and providing an answer that is coherent, articulate and cogent. Despite encouragement, their response can often simply be, 'I don't know.' The person may have difficulties with introspection (thinking about thoughts), which inhibits self-disclosure. Thus there may be a reluctance to disclose thoughts and feelings to colleagues and a line manager because 'When I talk to them it is so difficult to explain, and they just don't seem to understand me.'

An autistic person may not recognize that asking people to help, or to be part of their support team, can be useful in the workplace. There may be a lack of trust, where the person has experienced too many negative social interactions to feel confident that another person would be safe when disclosing information and the need for assistance.

Another difficulty associated with autism is not automatically perceiving people as a potential solution to problems. This is a very socially oriented way of thinking. Autistic people tend to feel more comfortable with a self-directed and solitary approach. If you tend to have difficulties with self-disclosure and seeking help, you may need guidance or careful reflection with Stages 2 and 5 when considering who is in your support team.

ACCOMMODATING PROBLEMS WITH SELF-DISCLOSURE AT WORK

- Reward yourself with a compliment whenever you put effort into disclosing your thoughts, feelings and reflections. Effort will yield results, and all effort deserves noticing and affirming.
- Take some time to type or write what you are thinking and need to disclose. This may enhance clarity of thought and help determine what to say and how to say it.
- If words are still elusive, create a drawing, or choose a scene in a film, or lyrics in a song, or use any another communication modality that may express your internal world.
- Think of logical reasons for the strategy of forming a support team. For example, two brains are better than one at solving problems – it doubles the data and brainpower available.

- When identifying your support team (see Stages 2 and 5), know that it is important to choose the right people, and consider the sort of traits or characteristics you would be looking for, for example, a person to whom you would feel comfortable disclosing your inner thoughts and feelings.

Specific learning or language difficulties

If you have a specific learning disorder such as dyslexia or dyscalculia, or English is your second language, further accommodations to the programme will need to be made.

ACCOMMODATING PROBLEMS WITH LEARNING OR LANGUAGE DIFFICULTIES

- Most of the pre-reading material for each stage is available for you to listen to as a video or audio recording.
- Use a translator or seek help from your mentor should English be your second language and the programme material is not easy to understand.
- Ask your mentor to sit with you and work through the material orally. Ask your mentor to provide explanations and interpretation for questions where these are needed.
- Multiple short stages to work on the programme material will be less exhausting than attempting a whole stage in one sitting.

Sensory perception

Most autistic people experience sensory issues, and by far the most experienced sensory issues are in relation to sounds and touch, that is, auditory sensitivity and tactile defensiveness. Specific sensory experiences range from being a source of distraction and agitation to being perceived as extremely painful and unbearable.

We recommend listing any major sensory issues prior to commencing the *Autism Working* programme:

_____

_____

_____

_____

ACCOMMODATING PROBLEMS WITH SENSORY PERCEPTION

- Set up the room you will be working in with consideration to background noise and unpredictable sounds such as incoming telephone calls, lighting sources and light intensity, aromas, your choice of clothing and comfort of the furniture.
- Use sensory or fidget toys as a calming and sensory blocking activity. If sensory toys are not available, sensory activities may include manipulating a small ball of Blu-Tack®, twiddling a pencil or gently rocking.

Difficulty conceptualizing and describing a sense of self

Autistic people often have difficulty with understanding and describing who they are, how they are thinking and how they are feeling, due to impaired _Theory of Mind_ abilities. _Theory of Mind_ refers to the intuitive ability to perceive, process and know the inner thoughts and feelings of another person's mind and one's own mind (self-reflection).

Autistic people can also struggle with autobiographical memory, that is, the ability to recall relevant details about their own life history to understand who they are and to therefore have an accurate self-understanding.

You may have a tendency to describe yourself in terms of your abilities and interests rather than your personality characteristics and social network. The concept of self from early childhood may also have been based on the rejection and criticisms of peers rather than the acceptance and compliments of peers.

This is one of the reasons that the _Autism Working_ programme provides so many resources, including information in print form and video recordings as well as questionnaires, to facilitate self-reflection and self-understanding as well as opportunities to seek other people's constructive opinions to contribute to achieving an accurate and positive concept of self that will be of benefit in the work environment.

ACCOMMODATING DIFFICULTIES WITH CONCEPT OF SELF

- If you are having difficulty completing the pre-course questionnaires before starting the programme, schedule an appointment with yourself in your diary to sit down and complete them all in one go or over two to three appointments, or find someone else to help complete the questionnaires who may know you well. Alternatively, find a mentor you can sit down with to complete the questionnaires together.
- Allow enough time for your own self-reflection. Remember, processing new information can take time. This will be important for your mentor to know.
- Validate and encourage yourself for any answers that you think about or write down. Approach each task with generosity toward yourself. Think: 'How can I really help myself here?' Please try to avoid being overly self-critical.
- Ensure all new self-insights and knowledge are recorded.

Stress Management Tools

We know from both research and clinical experience that people on the autism spectrum bring many awesome strengths to their work, and these include, amongst many:

- Attention to detail
- Loyalty
- Single-minded focus on the work task
- Extraordinary creativity
- High level of intellect
- Creative problem-solving capacity
- Sensory perception
- Strong work commitment
- High standard of work
- Ability to identify patterns and errors
- Knowledge.

We also know that there are some challenges that people on the autism spectrum face at work, and these include:

- Higher levels of stress than in the neurotypical population
- Social communication and social perspective problems, including recognizing the hierarchy at work, social chit-chat with colleagues and understanding oral multi-task instructions
- Problems with procrastination, prioritization and organization of time
- Challenges with daily living tasks, for example, a healthy sleep and eating routine
- A tendency to self-blame.

As part of this stage you will complete a questionnaire to identify your own strengths and difficulties, specific to the workplace (1.1 Strengths and Challenges within the Workplace). Considerable stress and anxiety arise when we do not understand our own profile of abilities. If we understand both our strengths and difficulties, we can use our strengths to overcome our difficulties.

There are two sections of material to read; the first describes the reasons for stress and anxiety in autistic people and the second describes tools to help you relax. You may now choose to read these sections or watch the videos instead (videos 1.1 and 1.2).

After reading this material, we will ask you to complete three additional questionnaires:

- 1.2 Identifying Our Own Signs of Stress and Anxiety
- 1.3 What Makes You Stressed?
- 1.4 DASS-21

It is important to learn the information presented in this stage and to watch the videos, as well as to complete the questionnaires, before completing the activities. The activities are designed to assist you to better manage the stress and anxiety that arises from work challenges.

⊙ The interplay between stress and autism
Genetics and neurology

You can read the following information or watch the video recording '1.1 The interplay between stress and autism'. Considerable research (see, for example, Ecker, Bookheimer and Murphy 2015) has identified a higher than expected prevalence of anxiety disorders in family members, both autistic and non-autistic. While there may be a genetic predisposition to high levels of anxiety, there is further research to suggest that there may also be a neurological reason for high levels of anxiety. Studies using neuroimaging technology of autistic adults identified structural and functional abnormalities of the amygdala, a part of the brain associated with the recognition and regulation of emotions, especially anxiety and fear. There is also research evidence to suggest a lack of neural connections between the amygdala and the frontal lobes of the brain.

A metaphor to help understand the function of the amygdala, anxiety and the frontal lobes is that of a vehicle being driven on a motorway. The frontal lobes of the brain are the driver, who makes executive decisions on what to do, where to go, etc. The amygdala functions as that part of the car dashboard that provides the driver with a warning signal regarding the temperature of the engine and the risk of 'overheating'. In the case of those who have autism, this part of their neurology, or 'dashboard', is not functioning with the degree of sensitivity of a typical emotion temperature gauge. Information on the increasing emotional heat and functioning of the engine is not available to the driver as a warning of impending overheating and the need to 'cool down'.

If you are unaware of your internal emotional state, then increasing levels of anxiety will be difficult to perceive and regulate. In autism, the dysfunction of the amygdala can also be expressed as a tendency to have a catastrophic emotional reaction at a relatively low threshold of anxiety, thereby pushing the 'panic button' too quickly. Neurotypical adults recognize signs of increasing anxiety much earlier and at a less intense level, and so are more easily able to manage their anxiety.

Sensory sensitivity

There are also environmental reasons for high levels of stress, related to heightened sensory sensitivity. Throughout the day, you may be exposed to extremely aversive and potentially overwhelming sensory experiences, such as colleagues shouting to each other in a noisy workplace, the aroma of a colleague's perfume or the smell of the toilet; tactile experiences, such as wearing protective clothing; or the glare and reflection from artificial lighting, especially fluorescent and downlighting.

Reading non-verbal communication

The diagnostic criteria for autism include difficulties reading non-verbal communication, and we recognize that if you have autism, you will have difficulty accurately reading the subtle, non-verbal cues that identify someone's feelings, and the depth of those feelings. However, autobiographies and our clinical experience suggest that when an autistic person perceives a negative emotion in another person, there is an oversensitivity to the negative emotion, especially anxiety, disappointment and agitation. As described by two autistic women, 'There's a kind of instant, subconscious reaction to the emotional states of other people that I have understood better in myself over the years', and 'If someone approaches me for a conversation and they are full of worry, fear or anger, I find myself suddenly in the same state of emotion.' Another adult said, 'Emotions are contagious for me.' Throughout the day there is a risk of being contaminated by the negative emotions of others and anxiety associated with not knowing when this is likely to occur; the experience will be extremely emotionally unpleasant and cause considerable stress.

Thinking style

We consider autism as a different way of perceiving, thinking, learning and relating. The thinking style can include an interest in discovering patterns and in particular, pattern breaks and errors. However, there can be considerable distress and anxiety if an error occurs that cannot easily be rectified. There can be an associated fear of making a mistake or performance anxiety, being determined not to make any errors.

There can also be a tendency for rigid or inflexible thinking, or a 'one-track' mind, and when change occurs requiring a new schedule, there can be considerable difficulty creating an internal representation of a new plan. Thus, if you have autism you may be very anxious anticipating or during unforeseen changes to daily routines and expectations in the workplace. There can be an insistence on sameness: variety is not the spice of life for all.

There are genetic, neurological, environmental and psychological reasons for high levels of stress in those who have autism, and problems with expressing and regulating emotions, particularly anxiety.

Increase in the characteristics of autism due to stress and anxiety

Stress and anxiety can also increase the core characteristics of autism, and some of the diagnostic characteristics of autism can be an attempt to manage anxiety. One of the diagnostic criteria is the presence of restricted, repetitive and ritualistic behaviours. However, these behaviours and actions may simply be self-soothing and function as a means of reducing anxiety, as occurs in the neurotypical population. Insistence on sameness is another diagnostic criterion that may occur to prevent experiencing situations known to create anxiety. The presence of special interests, another diagnostic criterion, may have many functions, including as a means of blocking anxious thoughts.

Stress and anxiety may also amplify other behaviours such as aggression, especially when attempts to reduce high levels of stress and anxiety are thwarted. Anxiety can also explain other behavioural characteristics associated with autism, such as acting as the 'rule policeman' – the person's attempt to reduce chaos and uncertainty in the workplace and impose order.

Common triggers for anxiety

Situations and events that can precipitate increasing anxiety may include:

- Disruptions to established routines
- Being expected to behave in a certain way, but not knowing how
- Being prevented from carrying out certain expected activities or routines
- Instances where there are too many demands and expectations
- The experience of social conventions and work rules and policies being broken
- Having a change imposed when not ready for it
- Having to wait or hurry up
- Fear of making a mistake or that a piece of work is not perfect
- Being considered stupid or incompetent by work colleagues or a line manager
- Making a literal interpretation of a comment intended to be encouraging, such as, 'You must always do your best'.

▶ Learning to relax

You can read the following information or watch the video recording '1.2 Learning to relax'. Learning to relax is a skill that we can develop. Many people on the autism spectrum seem to experience high levels of anxiety and stress as their default setting. The high levels are so unrelenting that it feels normal to be hyper-aroused and/or hypervigilant most of the time. We can also describe this state of being as the 'fight or flight mode'. Operating in this mode feels safe because it is a survival mode. Unfortunately, the 'fight or flight mode' is extremely tiring for the body and the mind. The adrenal glands are overstimulated and the mind state is generally pessimistic, sometimes to the point of developing into a depression. It can be difficult to sleep if we are always in 'fight or flight mode'. Racing thoughts and worries keep us awake, especially in the 'small hours'. It can also be difficult to trust other people, to see them as being potential allies or friends, or to accept their support or guidance.

The ideal state of being for activities such as relating to other people, learning new things, adapting to situations and being able to maintain productivity can be described as 'rest and digest mode'. When the body is in 'rest and digest mode', we have much greater capacity, and so can maintain work for longer. It is also enriching for our relationships, both at work and at home.

We highly recommend that, if you have not already found activities that you can regularly use to bring your body back into 'rest and digest mode', start finding these activities now, and practise using them regularly both at home and work. An important clue that your body has reached 'rest and digest' is that your heart rate will be beating at a steady, low to medium rate, your digestion will be working well, and you will not be sweating. Your breath will be calm and even. You will be breathing to the lower portion of your lungs rather than chest breathing, or the upper portion of your lungs.

Many activities can cause 'rest and digest mode'. To name a few, we find that drawing, listening to certain types of music, singing, being in nature, meditating, practising yoga, completing routine household or garden chores, being with a favourite pet, or reflecting on past happy experiences cause relaxation.

We highly recommend that you develop the ability to relax when you wish to. A method to enable you to do this has been developed by psychologists, drawing on knowledge of science, as well as ancient practices such as yoga. It is called progressive muscle relaxation (PMR). PMR is a technique that can be learned to assist us to relax when we need to. It is important to learn the skill of relaxation at times when we are already somewhat relaxed. Practising PMR in a quiet relaxing place teaches us to recognize the relaxation response in the body, and how to trigger that response. Once we are skilled at relaxing in a relaxing place, we can start applying the skills in stressful places, and when our stress response is triggered.

Questionnaires to complete now

Before you start the activities for this stage, you need to complete the following questionnaires. These will provide valuable information for you and your mentor (if you choose to have one) that you can apply when completing the activities that follow.

1.1 Strengths and Challenges within the Workplace Questionnaire

Challenges and strengths	1–5 scale
Dealing with emotion and stress	
I understand the specific work situations and other triggers that cause me anxiety, stress or depression	
I can identify my own anxiety, stress, depression or anger at low levels	
I can stay calm to manage emotions when they start to increase	
I understand my own sensory profile and know how to make the necessary accommodations	
I can cope with a meltdown at work	
I know ongoing strategies to assist with good mental health	
Looking after your body	
I have established a good physical exercise routine that keeps me feeling fit and healthy	
Most nights I can get to sleep easily and quickly	
I am able to manage my daily tasks well	
I eat a nourishing, healthy diet; I do not overeat or overindulge in junk food	
Social communication	
I have a good relationship with a mentor or colleague at work who can provide guidance and support	
I have a good relationship within my life outside work with someone with whom I can discuss problems	
I know my own capacity for socializing	
I can organize a social life that replenishes me and does not exhaust me	
I can communicate to family members, work colleagues and my line manager my increasing levels of anxiety or stress before these become a problem	
I have good assertiveness skills for the possibility of workplace bullying	

I can ask for help if I do not understand the instructions or my workplace tasks	
Looking after your mind	
In stressful situations I tend to approach the problem rather than avoid it	
I know my own vulnerabilities in the types of thoughts I have and have strategies for dealing with these	
I have effective problem-solving skills	
I have developed good strategies for managing my workload and organizing my time	
I can recognize when I procrastinate	
I can prioritize work tasks	
Other skills	
My energy levels are good	
I tend to feel alert and present most of the time	

Note: Using the scale 1–5, 1 indicates *no difficulty at all*, possibly a strength; 5 indicates *considerable difficulty.*

1.2 Identifying Our Own Signs of Stress and Anxiety Questionnaire

Please tick the signs of stress and anxiety that indicate to you that your stress and anxiety is becoming problematic and that it is time to do something about it.

Signs of stress and anxiety	Tick if applicable
Bodily sensations	
Sweaty palms and armpits	
Increased heart rate	
Fast breathing	
Muscle tension	
Sensations in the stomach	
'Goose bumps'	
Any other bodily sensations?	
Behaviours and actions	
Restlessness	
Fiddling with an object as a soothing activity	
The imposition of rituals and routines	
Avoiding change and spontaneity	
Social withdrawal	
A compulsion to engage in an action that acts as a thought-blocker	
Any other behaviours?	

Thoughts	
A lack of self-confidence	
Continual seeking of reassurance	
Reduced attention span, concentration and rigid thinking	
Racing thoughts	
In extreme situations, emotional meltdown	
Thinking that 'I can't do it'	
Being snappy	
Any other thoughts?	
Medical signs	
Changes in appetite	
Disruption of sleep	
Disturbances of the gastro-intestinal system, leading to constipation or diarrhoea	
Any other medical signs?	

1.3 What Makes You Stressed? Questionnaire

Tick the situations or triggers that apply to you, and add any other situations that you have recognized. Then rate the level of stress or anxiety from 0 to 10, with 10 being *extremely stressed or anxious*, and place that number in the box.

Situations or triggers for stress	Tick if applicable	0–10 scale
Sensory sensitivity		
Negative emotions in others		
Being criticized		
Making a mistake		
Disruptions to established routines		
Being expected to behave in a certain way, but not knowing how		
Times when prevented from carrying out certain expected activities or routines		
Instances where there are too many demands and expectations		
The experience of social conventions or work rules and policies being broken		
Having a change imposed when not ready for it		
Having to wait or hurry up		
Fear of making a mistake or work not being perfect		
Being considered stupid or incompetent by work colleagues or line manager		
Making a literal interpretation of a comment intended to be encouraging, such as, 'You must always do your best'		
Having to make 'small talk'		
Other situations		

1.4 Depression, Anxiety and Stress Scale-21 (DASS-21)

Autistic people can experience high levels of depression, anxiety and stress at times, and it is important to know if this is currently happening to you. High levels of depression, anxiety or stress will affect your sense of wellbeing, experience of work, and even your performance at work. Knowing your own stress, anxiety and depression levels is the first step in managing them.

Complete DASS-21 to ascertain your current levels of depression, anxiety and stress (Lovibond and Lovibond 1995). This is readily available for free online.[1] We will interpret your scores and what they mean in Activity 2.

---

1   Available at www2.psy.unsw.edu.au/dass

ACTIVITY 1: Understanding Your Strengths and Challenges

For this activity, you will need the questionnaire, 1.1 Strengths and Challenges within the Workplace, which you completed prior to starting this activity.

Take the questionnaire out now.

- Read your answers.
- Circle your key strengths and key difficulties.
- Decide what you wish to share with your mentor.

In the Introduction to the programme we recommended that you identify a mentor with whom you can discuss the activities and recommendations. Please discuss your answers to the questionnaire with your mentor. Share as much as you feel comfortable with, about your key strengths and your key challenges within the workplace.

Your personal notes from the discussion:

ACTIVITY 2: Knowing Your Current Levels of Depression, Anxiety and Stress

For this activity, score your completed DASS-21 and insert your scores below.

What were your levels?

_____ Depression   _____ Anxiety   _____ Stress

Using the table below, circle your own level of depression, anxiety and stress.

	Depression	Anxiety	Stress
Normal	0–4	0–3	0–7
Mild	5–6	4–5	8–9
Moderate	7–10	6–7	10–12
Severe	11–13	8–9	13–16
Extremely severe	14+	10+	17+

Share your current levels of depression, anxiety or stress with your mentor. This activity will assist you and your mentor in understanding the degree of support that you may need for managing any feelings of depression, anxiety or stress. If any of the levels are within the *severe* or *extremely severe* range, it may be wise to seek professional help from a clinical psychologist or psychiatrist.

Your personal notes from the discussion:

_____

_____

_____

_____

_____

_____

ACTIVITY 3: Understanding the Causes of Your Stress at Work

There can be many causes of stress at work. These can include:

- The workload (excessive or insufficient)
- Deadlines that may be unrealistic
- Having limited influence on what you are expected to do
- Limited understanding of the qualities and difficulties in the workplace for someone with autism
- Complex social dynamics and expectations
- New role requirements, policies and management
- Bullying and harassment
- Consistently achieving the required standard of work
- Workplace environment in terms of comfort and sensory experiences.

Which causes of workplace stress have you experienced? Circle those you have experienced from the list above.

Are there any other causes of stress that you have experienced?

_____

_____

_____

_____

With your mentor, discuss your causes of work stress.

Your personal notes from the discussion:

_____

_____

_____

_____

_____

ACTIVITY 4: Knowing Your Own Signs of Stress

We all experience stress; it is part of being human. We cannot rid you of stress, and we would never try to. However, sometimes our stress levels can be so high that our lives are negatively affected. Psychologically, there is a link between stress and anxiety. We become anxious when a situation may be unpleasant, and stress can be very unpleasant. Feeling stressed and anxious during and after work can lead to being emotionally exhausted, which can contribute to low self-esteem and feeling despondent or depressed. This could have a negative effect on work performance.

Prior to this component of Stage 1 you circled your own signs of anxiety that indicate to you that your anxiety is becoming problematic. Have a look at questionnaire 1.2 Identifying Our Own Signs of Stress and Anxiety.

Discuss with your mentor your personal signs of stress and anxiety that you recognize in your thinking, behaviour and actions.

Your personal notes from the discussion:

_____

_____

_____

_____

_____

_____

_____

_____

_____

_____

_____

_____

Using sports technology to measure how stressed you are feeling

The new sports and fitness technology devices worn on the wrist to measure heart rate can be used to record anxiety and stress levels throughout the day, and enable you to identify your stress and anxiety response to specific situations. This technology enables you to identify rising stress levels, signalling the need to communicate and manage them.

They can also be used to encourage the ability to relax, using a relaxation strategy such as breath control, where you are able to observe and respond to the gradual reduction in your heart rate, as shown on the screen of the device.

The devices are available from a range of stores, and we recommend that you visit a store that enables you to try out a range of devices that measure heart rate. Discuss with your mentor how useful such a device may be.

ACTIVITY 5: The Range of Situations at Work that Make You Stressed

You completed questionnaire 1.3 What Makes You Stressed? prior to starting the activities for Stage 1, rating your anxiety from 0 to 10, with 10 being *extremely stressed or anxious*. Please refer to this now.

With your mentor, explore the range of situations at work that make you stressed.

Your personal notes from the discussion:

_____

_____

_____

_____

_____

_____

_____

_____

_____

_____

_____

ACTIVITY 6: Strategies for Your Stressors at Work

Based on the previous discussion, write down one of the situations that causes you stress, followed by a list of ideas and strategies from yourself and your mentor that you could use to assist you to cope with that situation.

This is a situation or trigger that causes me stress:

_____

_____

_____

_____

_____

_____

_____

_____

Strategies can be divided into those that are helpful and those that are unhelpful.

In the spaces below, write down five to six helpful strategies for the situation you have described. Helpful strategies would include using skills such as: learn how to relax, think positive or helpful thoughts, take a break, seek solitude, or put the event into perspective. Reflect on your learning from the pre-reading and your discussions with your mentor to assist you.

Possible helpful strategies I could use:

_____

_____

_____

_____

_____

_____

_____

_____

_____

_____

_____

Unhelpful strategies may include: have a meltdown, say expletives, damage equipment, or avoid work or work tasks. We all use unhelpful strategies sometimes. Write down any strategies you may use that you have found to be unhelpful:

_____

_____

_____

_____

_____

_____

_____

_____

ACTIVITY 7: Energy Accounting

Maja Toudal from Denmark has ASD, and she originally created the concept of 'energy accounting' to help her identify situations that could be psychologically 'toxic' and drain her of energy, contributing to her feeling stressed and depressed and her cycles of exhaustion and depression. Part of this concept and associated strategies have been further developed and modified for this programme.

Imagine that in your mind you have an energy bank account, and throughout the day there are both withdrawals and deposits of energy. The following are possible withdrawals and deposits for someone who has autism:

Withdrawal	Deposit
• Socializing	• Solitude
• A change in routine or expectations	• Special interest
• Making a mistake	• Physical activity
• Sensory sensitivity	• Animals and nature
• Coping with anxiety	• Computer games
• Negative thoughts	• Sleep
• Crowds	• Drawing or being creative
• Being teased or excluded	• Reading
• Sensitivity to other people's moods	• Listening to music
• Over-analysing social performance	• Nutrition
• Crowds	• Mental health holiday
• Government agencies	• Information on the internet
• Body shape	• Being with pets
• Perceived injustice	• Meditation
• Certain people	• Caring for others
	• Certain people

The withdrawals and deposits would probably be very different for someone who does not have autism; for example, socializing and changes to routines and expectations may, for some people, be perceived as exciting and energizing.

In the following table, make a list of the typical daily withdrawals and deposits of energy in your work life in the activity/experience columns.

Ledger			
Energy account:			
Withdrawals		**Deposits**	
Activity/experience	**(0–100)**	**Activity/experience**	**(0–100)**

With energy accounting, we need a form of 'currency', that is, a numerical measure or value of how much an activity or experience drains or refreshes our energy from day to day.

The second part of this activity is to rate, from 0–100, the energy range of each activity or experience in your withdrawal or deposit columns. For example, on some days, socializing can drain you of energy at a value of around 20, but on other days it could be 100. The entry in the ledger above would therefore be 20–100. In the deposit column, on some days, listening to music would have an energizing value of 15, while on other days, a value of 40. Thus, the entry in the ledger would be 15–40.

You can use the Daily Energy Account Form (see below) to list the specific activities or experiences that were either an energy withdrawal or deposit on a particular work day. Write the value (0–100) of each of these activities to measure how draining or energizing they were. Then add all the numerical values in each of the two columns to see if your energy bank balance at the end of a day at work was in debit or credit, that is, in the black or in the red.

If your account was in the black, with more deposits than withdrawals, this is good energy accounting, and you will have reserves in your energy bank account to cope with subsequent energy-draining experiences over the next few days.

If the account is in the red, however, with more withdrawals than deposits, you will need to achieve more energy 'income' over the next few days. If you do not achieve a 'healthy' energy bank balance, the lack of energy in your account will increase the likelihood of both social and emotional problems.

Daily Energy Account Form

Date:			
Energy account:			
Withdrawals		**Deposits**	
Activity/experience	**(0–100)**	**Activity/experience**	**(0–100)**
Total:		Total:	
Closing balance (debit/credit):			
If necessary, what can I do tomorrow to compensate? How can I schedule more energy-infusing activities into my day?			

ACTIVITY 8: Progressive Muscle Relaxation

You have learned about PMR by reading the text earlier and/or watching the related video '1.2 Learning to relax'. To learn to do PMR, read Appendix A to understand the technique, then use the audio recording titled 'Progressive Muscle Relaxation' on the JKP library to guide your practice.

Start by practising PMR once per day during this programme. After one week of practice, start practising these skills by choosing one muscle group to tense and then relax during break times at work. It is important, however, to choose a muscle group that is not too obvious to others, for example, your leg, arm or hand muscles, rather than your face muscles. With regular practice, relaxation can become your natural response to stress triggers.

Recommended further reading for Stage 1

Attwood, T. and Garnett, M. (2016) *Exploring Depression, and Beating the Blues: A CBT Self-Help Guide to Understanding and Coping with Depression in ASD [ASD-Level 1]*. London and Philadelphia, PA: Jessica Kingsley Publishers.

Dubin, N. (2009) *Asperger Syndrome and Anxiety: A Guide to Successful Stress Management*. London and Philadelphia, PA: Jessica Kingsley Publishers.

Dubin, N. (2014) *The Autism Spectrum and Depression*. London and Philadelphia, PA: Jessica Kingsley Publishers.

Nason, B. (2019) *The Autism Discussion Page: On Stress, Anxiety, Shutdowns and Meltdowns: Proactive Strategies for Minimizing Sensory, Social and Emotional Overload*. London and Philadelphia, PA: Jessica Kingsley Publishers.

Wilkinson, L.A. (2015) *Overcoming Anxiety and Depression on the Autism Spectrum: A Self-Help Guide Using CBT*. London and Philadelphia, PA: Jessica Kingsley Publishers.

PERSONAL 'TAKE AWAYS' FROM STAGE 1

My three key strengths within the workplace are:

1. _____

2. _____

3. _____

My three key challenges in learning style within the workplace are:

1. _____

2. _____

3. _____

I experience significant _____ stress _____ anxiety _____ depression (please tick which apply).

My work stressors include:

1. _____

2. _____

3. _____

My Stress Management Tools for managing or reducing stress within the workplace are (circle the ones you believe will be most helpful to you):

1. Understanding Your Strengths and Challenges
2. Knowing Your Current Levels of Depression, Anxiety and Stress
3. Understanding the Causes of Your Stress at Work
4. Knowing Your Own Signs of Stress
5. Using Sports Technology to Monitor Your Signs of Stress
6. Strategies for Your Stressors at Work
7. Energy Accounting
8. Progressive Muscle Relaxation

Congratulations, you have now completed Stage 1!

Sensory Management Tools

⊛ Sensory perception and autism

You can read the following information or watch the video recording '2. Sensory perception and autism'.

We define autism primarily by the person's profile of abilities in the areas of social reasoning, language and cognitive abilities, but one of the attributes of autism, clearly identified in autobiographies and parents' descriptions of their children, and recognized in the DSM-5[1] diagnostic criteria for autism is a sensory perceptual system that works differently. These differences and how they impact on an autistic person are described below.

Some autistic adults consider their sensory sensitivity has a greater impact on their daily lives than problems with making friends, managing emotions and maintaining employment. Unfortunately, research studies have tended to ignore this aspect of autism, and we do not have a satisfactory explanation of why someone has an unusual sensory sensitivity or a range of effective strategies to modify sensory sensitivity.

The most common sensitivity is to specific sounds, but there can also be sensitivity to tactile experiences, light intensity, the taste and texture of food and specific aromas. There can be an under- or over-reaction to the experience of pain and physical discomfort, and the sense of balance, movement perception and body orientation can be unusual. One or several sensory systems can be affected such that everyday sensations are perceived as unbearably intense or apparently not perceived at all. Other people are often bewildered as to why these sensations are intolerable or not noticed,

---

1   *Diagnostic and Statistical Manual of Mental Disorders*, 5th Edition; see www.psychiatry.org/psychiatrists/practice/dsm

while the autistic person is equally bewildered as to why other people do not have the same level of sensitivity.

The autistic adult may genuinely notice sounds that are too faint for others to hear, is overly startled by sudden noises, or perceives sounds of a particular pitch (such as the sound of a hand-dryer or vacuum cleaner) as unbearable. The person is tempted to cover their ears to block out the sound or is desperate to get away from the specific noise. Bright sunlight can be almost 'blinding', specific colours are avoided as being too intense, and the person may notice and become transfixed by visual details, such as dust floating in a shaft of sunlight. There may be a self-imposed restricted diet that excludes food of a specific texture, taste, smell or temperature. Aromas such as perfumes or cleaning products can be avidly avoided because they cause the person to feel nauseous. There can also be problems with the sense of balance and the person may fear having their feet leave the ground and hate being upside down.

In contrast, there can be a lack of sensitivity to some sensory experiences, such as not responding to particular sounds, a failure to express pain when injured, an apparent lack of need for warm clothing in an extremely cold winter or perceiving the sensations of hunger and thirst. The sensory system can at one moment be hyper-sensitive and, in another moment, hypo-sensitive. However, some sensory experiences evoke intense pleasure, such as the sound and tactile sensation of a washing machine vibrating or the range of colours emitted by a streetlight.

An autistic person can have:

- Both hyper- and hypo-sensitivity to sensory experiences
- Sensory distortions
- Sensory 'tune-outs'
- Sensory overload
- Unusual sensory processing
- Difficulty identifying the source channel of sensory information.

Sound sensitivity

Three types of noise are perceived as extremely unpleasant. The first category is sudden, unexpected noises, the second is high-pitched, continuous sounds and the third is confusing, complex or multiple sounds. Some of these sounds can then be avoided. Silicone ear plugs can become a barrier to reduce the level of auditory stimulation.

Sensory overload

Autistic adults often describe feeling a sensation of sensory overload. The intense sensory experiences, or 'dynamic sensory surges' and overload, result in the autistic person being extremely stressed, anxious and almost 'shell shocked' in situations that are not perceived as aversive but enjoyable for others. The person with sensory sensitivity becomes hypervigilant, tense and distractible in sensory-stimulating environments, unsure when the next painful sensory experience will occur. They may actively avoid specific situations such as corridors, lunchrooms or the cafeteria, the factory floor, busy shopping centres and supermarkets, which are known to be too intense a sensory experience.

The fearful anticipation can become so severe that an anxiety disorder can develop, such as a phobia of dogs, because they might suddenly bark, or agoraphobia (fear of public places), as home is a relatively safe and controlled sensory experience. Some social situations such as attending a work party may be avoided, not only because of uncertainty regarding the expected social conventions, but also because of the noise levels.

Exploring your own sensory profile

Next please complete the following questionnaire, 2.1 Sensory Perception (Tavassoli, Hoekstra and Baron-Cohen 2014). The results will assist you to explore further your own sensory perception and specifically, where the challenges are.

2.1 Sensory Perception

Please tick those items that describe your sensory perception.

Sensory perception	Tick if applicable
I am able to distinguish different people by their smell	
I am able to detect if a strawberry is ripe by smell alone	
I am able to visually detect the change in brightness of a light each time a dimmer control is moved one notch	
I would notice if someone added 5 drops of lemon juice to my cup of water	
I would be able to hear a leaf move if blown by the wind on a quiet street	
I would be able to taste the difference between two brands of salty potato crisps	
I am able to feel the label at the back of my shirt	
I can hear electricity humming in the walls	
I notice the flickering of a desktop computer, even when it is working properly	
I would be able to notice a tiny change (such as 1 degree) in the temperature of the weather	
I would be able to feel a one millimetre cut in my skin	
I would be able to tell the weight difference between two different coin sizes on the palm of my hand, if my eyes were closed	
I could distinguish a familiar person and a stranger by their smell	
I can detect if bread is stale purely by its smell	
I would be able to detect the sound of a vacuum cleaner from any room in a two-storey building	
I would be able to feel the elastic holding up my socks if I stop and thought about it	
I would be able to taste the difference between apparently identical sweets	
I notice the weight and pressure of a hat on my head	

I would feel if a single hair touched the back of my hand	
If I was walking along, I would be able to feel a passing truck's vibrations even if my eyes were closed	
I would be able to smell the smallest gas leak from anywhere in the house	
I wouldn't notice if someone changed their perfume by smell alone	
I can't go out in bright sunlight without sunglasses	
I would be able to feel a change in the temperature of a cup of coffee after it had sat for 1 minute	
I would be the first to hear if there was a fly in the room	
If I look at a pile of blue jumpers in a shop that are meant to be identical, I would be able to see differences between them	
I wouldn't detect a new smell in my house instantly before anyone else	
I would be able to smell the difference between most men and women	
I would be able to hear each note in a chord even if there were 10 notes	
I close curtains to avoid bright lights	
I would be able to distinguish two brands of coffee by their smell, even with my eyes closed	
I can see dust particles in the air in most environments	
I would be able to taste the difference between two brands of tomato sauce if they had different concentrations of salt	
I would be able to smell the smallest amount of burning from anywhere in the house	
If my mobile phone was vibrating in my pocket, I would be quick to sense it	
How many of the 35 have you circled?	

ACTIVITY 1: Exploring Your Sensory Perception

With your mentor, and using the questionnaire items you endorsed to guide you, discuss the categories of sensory perception associated with autism to which you are sensitive, such as touch, hearing, vision, smell and taste, and the subcategories of pressure, temperature, pain and vibration.

There may be other aspects of sensory perception such as a reduced sensitivity to hunger, thirst, bodily sensations, and the onset of being ill and proprioception, the awareness of the body in space and the sense of balance controlled by the vestibular system.

The discussion can include describing the degree of discomfort, if not acute pain, when perceiving specific sensory experiences, and how sensory sensitivity affects concentration and can contribute to feeling stressed and anxious.

There is also the issue of whether the degree of sensory sensitivity is appreciated and accommodated by colleagues and your line manager, and the value of communicating your sensory sensitivity to others in the workforce. You can discuss with your mentor how to explain you sensory sensitivity to colleagues and your line manager.

Your personal notes from the discussion:

_____

_____

_____

_____

_____

_____

_____

_____

_____

_____

Coping with sensory sensitivity

There are two types of coping mechanisms with overwhelming sensory experiences: personal coping strategies and environmental accommodations.

Personal coping strategies require you to make some adjustment, either physical or psychological, to accommodate the sensory experience. Examples include:

- Creating a barrier such as wearing ear plugs or considering Irlen lenses to reduce visual sensitivity and distortion
- Being brave and enduring the experience
- Creating a sensory repair kit that could include peppermint oil drops on a handkerchief to camouflage an unpleasant smell, your mobile phone so you can listen to music or a podcast using noise-cancelling headphones as a barrier to aversive auditory sensations and fidget toys as a temporary distraction.

Environmental accommodations will require your employer, line manager or work colleagues to agree to reasonable changes to your workplace. Examples include:

- Moving your desk away from the source of an irritating noise, such as a refrigerator or machinery
- Making changes to the lighting, from fluorescent to incandescent or natural lighting
- Asking other staff members to turn off or lower the volume of music or the radio.

ACTIVITY 2: Strategies to Cope with Sensory Sensitivity

With your mentor, complete the table below to identify personal coping strategies and environmental accommodations that you could request at work.

Sensory experience	Personal coping strategy	Environmental accommodation
Sounds		
Visual		
Smell		
Touch		
Taste		

Sensory meltdown

A sensory meltdown can occur when you feel that you are experiencing sensory overload and the intensity of sensory experiences become unbearable and you are rapidly losing the ability to remain calm and have a desperate need to escape the situation.

ACTIVITY 3: Your Personal Experiences of Sensory Meltdowns

Either contemplate and make notes or discuss with your mentor the answers to the following questions:

- What are your signs of an imminent meltdown?
- What strategies could be used to prevent a meltdown?
- How can you recover?
- How can your colleagues help you before, during and after a sensory meltdown?

Your personal notes from the discussion:

Recommended further reading for Stage 2

Bogdashina, O. (2020) *Sensory Perceptual Issues in Autism and Asperger Syndrome: Different Sensory Experiences – Different Perceptual Worlds.* London and Philadelphia, PA: Jessica Kingsley Publishers.

Hefferman, D. (2016) *Sensory Issues for Adults with Autism Spectrum Disorder.* London and Philadelphia, PA: Jessica Kingsley Publishers.

PERSONAL 'TAKE AWAYS' FROM STAGE 2

Sensory challenges affect me at work in these ways:

1. _____

2. _____

3. _____

My three key personal strategies for managing difficult sensory experiences at work are:

1. _____

2. _____

3. _____

These three changes to the environment at work would really help me focus:

1. _____

2. _____

3. _____

Congratulations, you have now completed Stage 2!

Social Tools

▶ Social difficulties and autism

You can read the following information or watch the video recording '3. Social difficulties and autism'.

The characteristics of autism include difficulty achieving social reciprocity, reading non-verbal communication and developing teamwork skills. This can lead to problems at work with social communication. Further difficulties can arise because autistic people tend to be primarily motivated to achieve work goals, for example, getting the job done to a high standard and finalizing the details, whereas neurotypical people often focus to a greater extent on social goals, for example, relating to someone, being liked, receiving compliments, pleasing others, etc. Both sets of goals are important and valid in a work setting, but these goals need to be balanced and appropriate for the work environment. Problems can arise when a person on the autism spectrum in the workplace does not realize their own role and contribution to social communication breakdowns, and when the work culture does not understand or embrace the characteristics and motivations of the person who has autism. It is important at work to recognize that it takes two to make a social interaction successful.

Social Tools refers to strategies that make successful social communication more likely. These include being able to:

- Access social guidance in the workplace
- Effectively use social communication scripts
- Know strategies for repair when social communication breaks down
- Assertively and effectively manage workplace bullying.

ACTIVITY 1: Identifying and Understanding Your Personality Qualities

One of the best assets you have for using social tools at work is your *personality*, and in particular, your personality strengths. This activity is designed to assist you to recognize your personality qualities, and we will then start to see how these strengths can enhance your social communication at work.

Your personality can be conceptualized as a piece of a jigsaw puzzle. Each person has a unique personality or jigsaw 'shape'. Some shapes fit other shapes easily while some people have unusual characteristics (or jigsaw shapes) and must adjust their characteristics to more easily 'fit in', or search for another matching shape.

Some personality qualities are needed for specific jobs, such as relating to customers or the ability to work effectively in a team. Exploring your personality characteristics can help you discover personality qualities that can be beneficial at work and when making friends or in a relationship.

Personality qualities are those characteristics that describe who you are, such as being kind, helpful, loyal, resilient, non-judgemental, supportive, determined, trustworthy, thoughtful, honest, self-confident, intelligent, quiet, cheerful or generous, or having a sense of humour or a vivid imagination. These are just some of the many hundreds of words used to describe someone's personality.

We have listed below some positive personality adjectives. Circle the characteristics that describe your personality.

Adventurous	Considerate
Affectionate	Courageous
Ambitious	Courteous
Articulate	Creative
Artistic	Curious
Careful	Dependable
Cheerful	Determined
Compassionate	Easy-going

Empathic

Energetic

Enthusiastic

Fair

Forgiving

Friendly

Funny

Generous

Gentle

Helpful

Honest

Imaginative

Inventive

Kind

Loyal

Mischievous

Neat

Persistent

Polite

Practical

Proud

Quick-witted

Quiet

Rational

Reliable

Reserved

Serious

Shy

Silly

Sincere

Studious

Sympathetic

Thoughtful

Tolerant

Tidy

Trusting

Wise

ACTIVITY 2: Understanding Your Personality Qualities as Strengths in the Workplace

Take time to think about how each of your personality qualities can be an advantage at work in terms of:

- **R**elationships with your customers or clients, colleagues and manager/s
- **S**elf-esteem and self-identity
- **E**njoying success in your working life.

Next to the quality you have circled, place an **R**, **S** or **E**, as defined above, to denote how the quality could be beneficial in each area of life. Some of your qualities may have all three work advantages.

ACTIVITY 3: How Your Personality Qualities Can Be an Advantage

Discuss with your mentor your thoughts on how your personality qualities can be an advantage in your working life now and in the future. Make notes below on how your qualities are an advantage in each of the three areas.

1. Relationships at work

_____

_____

_____

_____

2. Self-esteem and self-identity

_____

_____

_____

_____

3. Enjoyment of success in your working life

_____

_____

_____

_____

ACTIVITY 4: Understanding Potential Difficulties with Social Communication at Work

Remember that successful social communication requires all participants in a social interaction to understand each other's perspective, motivation and social abilities. The following potential difficulties are divided into problems you may have experienced within yourself and problems you may have experienced with other people.

Take a moment now to consider any social communication difficulties you have experienced at work, and consider the following difficulties with social communication.

Social communication difficulties	Tick which apply
I have had difficulty:	
Being able to ask for help when I need it	
Being able to offer strategies for repair of the interaction when communication breaks down	
Being able to assertively manage workplace bullying	
Understanding another person's point of view or objectives	
Taking a literal interpretation when this was not intended	
I find other people at work difficult when:	
They expect more socializing than I think is needed or I can cope with, such as superficial chit-chat, talking about uninteresting or irrelevant topics	
They do not seem to appreciate an honest answer to their question	
They interrupt my work and/or conversation	
They do not understand my point of view, even after I explain it many times	

Have any of these ever happened to you? Can you foresee that any of these could happen to you? Can you think of any other social communication difficulties that may come up for you at work? Discuss the actual and potential social communication difficulties that arise with your mentor and make notes below.

Your personal notes from the discussion:

_____

_____

_____

_____

_____

_____

_____

_____

_____

_____

_____

_____

_____

_____

ACTIVITY 5: Accessing Social Support When You Need It

One of the problems with trying to solve social communication problems on our own is that we are too close to the problem to see it clearly. A colleague or your mentor can be invaluable to assist you to see the problem from another point of view, which then has good potential to lead to a solution.

Can you think of a time when someone in your life helped you to resolve a social communication problem? This may have been a parent, friend or teacher.

Discuss with your mentor how other people have been an excellent resource to resolve social communication problems.

Your personal notes from the discussion:

ACTIVITY 6: Creating a Social Support Network

Please look at the diagram in Appendix B. There are a number of people who could be involved in your social support network. Here is a list of possible people and their roles:

Role of each person in your social support network

HR manager

This person is responsible for recruitment, identifying a need for workplace accommodations for an individual or work group, and providing advice to managers regarding workplace policies and any interpersonal disputes or grievances.

Line manager

A person with direct managerial and work productivity responsibility for an employee, often responsible for making decisions regarding work tasks, prioritization, providing feedback and performance appraisal and implementing workplace accommodations.

Workplace mentor

A senior or more experienced employee who is assigned to act as an advisor in the workplace and guides or trains an employee. Workplace mentors monitor work abilities and performance.

Autism work consultant or coach

This person monitors the support requirements of an autistic individual at work and provides advice on strategies to facilitate successful employment.

Psychologist

An expert or specialist in psychology, this person will often be external to the organization you work for, but can be useful when needed to support an individual to deal with issues such as stress, anxiety and depression and acquiring specific social abilities.

Partner, parent, sibling or friend

This person may be able to help you understand some of the social dynamics and issues in the workplace and offer advice on how to manage specific social situations. They will have considerable knowledge of your social abilities and challenges and how to acquire specific skills and social scripts.

Take some time now to identify for yourself who would be the best people in your work life to offer you guidance and advice about social situations and social communication at work.

Write down the names of the following people who may be part of your social support network at work.

HR manager:

Line manager:

Workplace mentor:

Autism work consultant or coach:

Write down the names of people in your home or personal life who may be part of your social support network for difficulties with social communication at work.

Partner, parent or sibling:

Friend:

Psychologist, counsellor or life coach:

▶ Sharing information with your support team

As you know from the Introduction, there are three videos that we have prepared for your support team that are available on the JKP Library. These three videos are: 'What is ASD?', 'How do I work productively with a person with ASD in the workplace?' and 'Social communication and ASD in the workplace'. Watch these videos now with your mentor.

ACTIVITY 7: Your Social Support Network

Discuss the following points with your mentor:

- What you need to tell each person in your social support network about any difficulties at work with social communication and how this would differ depending on the person's role.
- If any video or part of the video would be helpful for anyone in your support team to view.

What are the potential barriers that may come up for you that could prevent you from seeking social support when it is needed? These could include being able to identify a breakdown in social communication, reading someone's intentions or 'hidden agenda', being reluctant to disclose times of social confusion, and so on:

_____

_____

_____

_____

_____

_____

Discuss some potential solutions to these barriers. These could include arranging a time to discuss any difficulties you may have with social communication and preparing notes to be used during the discussion:

_____

_____

_____

_____

_____

ACTIVITY 8: Developing Social Scripts for Social Communication Breakdown

With an insight into problems with social communication and motivation to repair any problems, we have found that it is possible to use social scripts to manage a breakdown in social communication. Social scripts can be useful for most of the social communication difficulties outlined in this programme.

Consider the following questions based on potential difficulties in social situations and, with your mentor, create a script for each situation. Also consider how you would communicate this differently to different people at work, for example, your line manager or work colleagues. Your mentor may be able to provide some insight and advice.

How could you communicate that you prefer to be alone during lunch breaks and do not want to talk to your line manager and colleagues?

Line manager:

_____

_____

Colleagues:

_____

_____

How could you communicate that you sometimes interrupt others while they are having a conversation, but that you do not mean to be rude or offend others?

Line manager:

_____

_____

Colleagues:

_____

_____

How could you communicate that you want to end the social conversation and get back to work?

Line manager:

_____

_____

Colleagues:

_____

_____

How could you communicate that you are very upset by a critical comment?

Line manager:

_____

_____

Colleagues:

_____

_____

How would you make an apology if it seems that someone is offended by what you said, even if you did not mean offence?

Line manager:

_____

_____

Colleagues:

_____

_____

Consider a problem in social communication that you have experienced in the past. Would a social script help? Formulate a script with your mentor that you may be able to use in the future should the problem arise again.

Line manager:

_____

_____

Colleagues:

_____

_____

ACTIVITY 9: Role-Playing Scripts for Social Communication Repair

Your mentor can guide you through a role-play of a situation that you have identified as a potential problem, to give you the opportunity to practise one or more of your scripts. Prior to engaging in the role-play, consider the delivery of your script, and also:

- What is the intention of the social communication?
- What facial expressions should you make?
- What tone of voice will maximize the possibility of success?
- What body posture and gestures would be appropriate?

After the role-play, your mentor will give you feedback and advice on what you said and how you said it. Please make notes on the key learning points from your perspective:

Social scripts and role-plays

Sometimes using a script does not have the desired effect, and the social communication problem continues. If you have trialled all the strategies available to you, including creating scripts and role-playing the script, and have managed any background emotions that could affect the delivery of the script, and yet the problem with social communication is still there, we highly recommend that you use a person in your social support network to determine further strategies. Sometimes someone outside the problem may be able to help you to develop further self-insight or insight into the problem, as well as develop a new idea about what to do. In other cases, a mediation process at work may be helpful.

You may need to explain to your employer and colleagues any difficulties that you may have with:

- Processing long and complex instructions
- Literal interpretation of a comment
- Transitioning to a new activity
- Fine and gross motor skills
- An unusual sense of humour
- Coping with sarcasm
- Responding with an empathic comment
- Recognizing personal space
- Being touched
- A tendency to repeatedly correct someone's errors
- Using excessive technical details and being pedantic
- Knowing how to start and end a conversation
- Understanding office politics and interpersonal dynamics
- Being honest but causing embarrassment
- Understanding appropriate dress sense and personal hygiene
- Emotional attachment
- Gossip
- Flirting.

It may be valuable to create scripts that are rehearsed in role-plays to explain a range of difficulties that an autistic person can have in the workforce.

Strategies for being bullied, teased, rejected and ridiculed

Unfortunately, autistic people are more likely to be the target of bullying, teasing, rejection and ridicule than neurotypical work colleagues. The psychological consequences can be a major contributor to increasing stress and feeling depressed and anxious at work.

There are seven types of bullying:

- Verbal: Making derogatory comments, embarrassing remarks or making fun of your abilities or personality
- Physical: Pushing or shoving you, taking things from you
- Emotional: Practical jokes, malicious gossip, mocking
- Intimidating: Making threats, being aggressive and creating a feeling of fear
- Sexual: Being touched on areas of the body that you consider are private, asking you to dress in ways that you do not like
- Cyber: Posting misinformation, rumours or insulting comments about you online
- Financial: Getting you to pay for things you do not want to, borrowing money and not repaying you.

Those who engage in bullying are often good at finding your sensitive topic or personal weakness. They usually target someone who is often alone and lacks self-confidence and protection from colleagues.

Their motivations can be:

- Becoming 'top dog' or 'queen bee' in the workforce
- Valuing being aggressive as a positive personality trait
- Despising someone who is different or may have greater work skills
- To get what they want from you
- To make others laugh.

ACTIVITY 10: Identifying Strategies for Being Bullied

Discuss with your mentor strategies to reduce the likelihood of being bullied, teased, socially rejected or ridiculed at work. It is important to discuss how you should not react and what would be a wise reaction, and how to be clear and assertive in what you say.

Wise reactions can include:

- After an incident, recording in detail the circumstances, participants and sequence of events, behaviours and comments as well as the effect on you and your work performance – you need evidence of what happened
- Seeking guidance, verification and validation from a work colleague
- Ensuring you have an opportunity to emotionally 'de-brief' with someone you trust in the workforce or at home
- Creating and rehearsing with that person or your mentor an assertive response, should such an incident happen again
- Creating thoughts that could be used during and after the incident to maintain being calm and reducing your emotional reaction
- Knowing your employer's policies and procedures for such incidents and who to contact in the organization regarding such actions. Remember that the consequences of bullying in the workplace can lead to decreased work performance and the resignation of people who are an asset to their employer
- Ignoring it (if you can) but trying not to be visibly distressed or angry
- Asking the person to stop in an assertive manner.

Any other suggestions:

_____

_____

_____

_____

_____

_____

Recommended further reading for Stage 3

Gallup, S. (2017) *Making Friends at Work: Learning to Make Positive Choices in Social Situations for People with Autism*. London and Philadelphia, PA: Jessica Kingsley Publishers.

Grandin, T. and Barron, S. (2017) *Unwritten Rules of Social Relationships: Decoding Social Mysteries Through the Unique Perspectives of Autism*. Arlington, TX: Future Horizons, Inc.

Jordan, P. (2017) *How to Start, Carry On and End Conversations: Scripts for Social Situations for People on the Autism Spectrum*. London and Philadelphia, PA: Jessica Kingsley Publishers.

Tickle, A. and Stott, B. (2010) *Exploring Bullying with Adults with Autism and Asperger Syndrome*. London and Philadelphia, PA: Jessica Kingsley Publishers.

PERSONAL 'TAKE AWAYS' FROM STAGE 3

My three key strategies for managing being bullied, teased, rejected and ridiculed within the workplace are:

1. _____

2. _____

3. _____

My top three social communication difficulties within the workplace are:

1. _____

2. _____

3. _____

My three key strategies for seeking social support within the workplace are:

1. _____

2. _____

3. _____

My three key strategies for managing social communication difficulties at work are:

1. _____

2. _____

3. _____

Congratulations, you have now completed Stage 3!

Awareness Tools

Self-awareness, meditation and autism

There are many types of awareness, and we are specifically focusing on self-awareness in this stage. One of the key ways we can increase our self-awareness is to practise meditation. You may be wondering why we chose to include meditation in a programme to enhance your work skills. The answer, in a nutshell, is that there is now over 40 years of research to show that establishing a regular meditation practice is not only good for one's physical and mental health, but has also been shown to be very powerful for increasing a person's self-awareness, and thus their self-regulation and social abilities, as well as their performance at work. We also know through research that the very areas of the brain that are affected by autism, and that cause the challenges of autism, are the areas that brain morphology studies show are positively affected by meditation (Fox *et al.* 2014).

Many types of meditation are available. Some involve noticing your thoughts, for example, mindfulness meditation, and others involve clearing the mind of thoughts. For the purpose of this programme we have chosen to use Sahaja yoga meditation because there is good research to show increased self-awareness using this meditative practice at the rate of once per day for 10 minutes (Manocha 2016). Sahaja yoga meditation involves learning how to clear the mind of thoughts. This is not to say that thoughts will magically vanish, but you will be practising how to let your thoughts go, that is, to not give them so much of your time and energy. Acquiring this skill is very useful for autistic people because they tend to worry and ruminate a lot, which is exhausting and generally unhelpful.

Some autistic people find meditation very difficult to do, to the point of stopping after only a few trials. This is true of three groups especially, and it is worth understanding which group you may be in, if this is your experience.

The first group includes those people who have extreme sensory sensitivity. When they practise meditation, they find it difficult to sit with certain uncomfortable sensory experiences of hearing certain noises, or other sensory stimuli. If you are in this group, we recommend practising noticing the sensations that are more difficult or aversive, and noticing how your mind reacts to these sensations. Notice any thoughts, feelings and bodily sensations. Next notice any *other* sensory experiences that are occurring. Bring these to the foreground, and then go back to the original difficult sensation. Rotate your attention between the various sensory experiences available to you, and then let all of them go, and bring awareness to the space above your head, as in the directions from Sahaja yoga meditation. If this is all too difficult, we recommend engaging a psychologist or occupational therapist to assist with managing the extreme sensory sensitivity. There are many methods to help from these professions. If sensory sensitivity is getting in the way of meditation, it will also likely interfere with your working life, so it is worth getting help.

The second group of people who find meditation difficult includes those who use suppression and avoidance, including thought-blocking activities, such as incessant screen use, alcohol and other drugs, and mobile phone checking, to avoid their thoughts and feelings. For these people, when they stop to meditate, all the thoughts and feelings they have been suppressing, avoiding and blocking rush into the mind with the force of a freight train. The pressure of the rushing thoughts can feel very disorienting and aversive. If you are in this group, our recommendation is to stay with it and 'buckle in for the ride'. Practise noticing the thoughts as they rush in, a bit like watching a rollercoaster whoosh by, but not climbing on to feel all the turmoil. Know that it will stop; the secret is not to engage in it. The torrent is only thoughts and feelings and they cannot hurt you. They will slow and eventually stop. Just allow the process to work. If it is too disorienting or difficult, keep coming back to a part of your body that feels safe and grounded during the process; for example, plant the heels of your feet into the floor and feel grounded to the earth. If this doesn't work, please consult a psychologist. Psychologists have specialist training to assist with managing persistent disorienting and distressing thoughts. Working out ways to process the suppressed thoughts will free up energy for productivity and wellbeing, and give you better sleep too.

Lastly, the third group who find stilling the thoughts in the mind difficult are those for whom trauma, either a single event, or complex trauma, has been part of their life experience. In this case, not only can suppressed thoughts come up, but also unwanted disturbing images, strong emotions and bodily sensations related to past trauma. If this is the case for you, we strongly recommend consulting a psychologist with training in trauma and autism. Unfortunately, traumatic incidents are common for autistic people, and symptoms of traumatic stress do not go away by themselves. The good news is that traumatic stress reactions are treatable. It is worth pursuing this option to decrease the other symptoms that come along with trauma and that will interfere with work, including high levels of physiological arousal, insomnia, depression, nightmares, flashbacks, distrust of others and dissociation.

If you already have a meditation practice, we encourage you to continue with it. You are also very welcome to trial this particular yoga meditation throughout this course. To teach you meditation in this course we will be using free resources on the Beyond the Mind website.[1]

Whilst meditation is a powerful Awareness Tool, it is not the only one. People use many strategies to help keep them focused and aware of both their body and the environment on a moment-by-moment basis. The key to a meditation practice is that the activity is conducted with the intention of noticing both internal and external information at the same time, continuously, without becoming 'hooked' on a source of information other than the chosen focus. Being able to meditate is skill that takes practice.

The first step is attention training – training our mind to focus on the meditation, even though other things will distract us. The next step is acceptance – accepting that this is difficult. The last step is to be compassionate with oneself whilst practising meditation and having difficulty with focusing the mind.

Other potential Awareness Tools apart from meditation include: yoga, martial arts, mindfulness practices, art, learning a musical instrument, gardening, being in nature, sailing, and any other practice that calms your physiology, keeps you in the moment, and thus gives your mind a break from unhelpful patterns of thought.

---

1   www.beyondthemind.com

ACTIVITY 1: Understanding Meditation

Information about the specific meditation practice we wish to share with you is provided on the Beyond the Mind website, under the tab 'How to Meditate'. All of the information presented here is valuable, but if you are short of time we particularly recommend that you read the information under the tabs 'What Am I Aiming to Experience?' and 'Basic Meditation'.

ACTIVITY 2: Meditation Practice

Engage in the 10-minute 'Meditation' practice as described on the Beyond the Mind website under the tab 'How to Meditate'. If you would like to try with an audio recording, we have created one which we share on the JKP Library website.

With your mentor, describe your reactions to the 'Meditation' activity, including answering questions such as:

- What did you experience?
- Did you find the exercise relaxing?
- Did you experience any moments of lack of thought, or thoughtless awareness?
- Did you experience this exercise as stressful?

Most people who experience this 'Meditation' activity can achieve thoughtless awareness for at least a few moments; however, some people take more than two to three sessions to achieve this state. There is no right or wrong response.

Please record your initial thoughts on meditation here:

_____

_____

_____

_____

_____

_____

_____

We encourage you to practise 'Meditation' for 10 minutes every day. Besides many physical and mental health benefits you will also increase your sense of awareness of yourself and others, leading to increased capacity to face the challenges and problems within your workplace.

Recommended further reading for Stage 4

Bolls, U.D. (2013) *Meditation for Aspies: Everyday Techniques to Help People with Asperger Syndrome Take Control and Improve their Lives*. London and Philadelphia, PA: Jessica Kingsley Publishers.

Goodchild, C. (2017) *Unclouded by Longing: Meditations on Autism and Being Present in an Overwhelming World*. London and Philadelphia, PA: Jessica Kingsley Publishers.

Harris, R. (2017) *Contemplative Therapy for Clients on the Autism Spectrum: A Reflective Integration Therapy™ Manual for Psychotherapists and Counsellors*. London and Philadelphia, PA: Jessica Kingsley Publishers.

Manocha, R. (2016) *Silence Your Mind*. Sydney, NSW: Hachette.

Mitchell, C. (2008) *Asperger's Syndrome and Mindfulness: Taking Refuge in the Buddha*. London and Philadelphia, PA: Jessica Kingsley Publishers.

Mitchell, C. (2008) *Mindful Living with Asperger's Syndrome: Everyday Mindfulness Practices to Help You Tune in to the Present Moment*. London and Philadelphia, PA: Jessica Kingsley Publishers.

PERSONAL 'TAKE AWAYS' FROM STAGE 4

Awareness Tools I currently use or could begin to use include:

1. _____

2. _____

3. _____

Barriers to practising meditation:

1. _____

2. _____

3. _____

Strategies to help me to develop a daily meditation practice:

1. _____

2. _____

3. _____

My support team can help me in the following ways:

1. _____

2. _____

3. _____

Congratulations, you have now completed Stage 4!

Thinking Tools

▶ Recognizing and challenging your unhelpful thinking patterns

You can read the following information or watch the video recording '5. Recognizing and challenging your own thinking patterns'.

Although we cannot change some situations, we do have some control over how we feel and react to them, and through our thoughts and actions we can repair our feelings of anxiety, stress and/or depression. In other words, the way we think about a situation determines in large part how we feel about that situation.

If we have awareness of our thinking patterns, we have a choice. Unfortunately, when we are tired, anxious, angry, stressed or depressed, our automatic or default thinking style tends to be pessimistic; thus, our thoughts can actually keep us anxious and stressed if we let them. The trick is to recognize this pattern of thinking and not believe your first or pessimistic thought.

From our extensive clinical experience with adults who have autism, we want to stress how important self-awareness is for recognizing and interrupting unhelpful thinking patterns. Without self-awareness, unhelpful thinking patterns happen quite automatically, and the resulting rush of negative emotion can be very difficult to manage.

Common unhelpful thinking patterns

Professor Aaron Beck, now considered the 'father' of cognitive behaviour therapy, was the first to identify common thinking patterns that can lead to getting 'stuck' in strong unhelpful states of mind (1975). We include these in our programme because there is considerable evidence to show that identifying and challenging our unhelpful or self-defeating thoughts is an extremely useful tool for staying calm and mentally clear at work and at home.

The more often we reflect on and challenge our habitual unhelpful patterns of thinking, the more quickly we learn to challenge our thinking distortions and stop believing the error messages. The result is that we experience increased feelings of wellbeing and calm, leading to better decision-making at work and in life in general.

There are many different Thinking Tools that you can use to enhance your work experience and daily life. In this stage of *Autism Working*, we will describe and explore the Thinking Tools that are most useful to stay grounded, being realistic and mentally calm and clear.

ACTIVITY 1: Understanding the Connection between Thinking and Feeling

Imagine this situation:

> You are waiting at the cafeteria at work for your new work colleague, Matt, to arrive to have lunch together. You are supposed to meet at 12.30 pm. It is now 1 pm and there is no sign of Matt.

Person A starts to think: 'What did I do wrong last time I spoke to Matt? He seemed fine and agreed to have lunch together, but now he has not turned up. I just know he no longer likes me. Just like all the other times I have tried to make a friend. I will never make a friend. I am hopeless and unlikeable. There is just something terribly wrong with me.'

How is person A feeling?

_____

_____

_____

Why do you think he or she feels this way?

_____

_____

_____

What is the evidence for the thought 'I am hopeless and unlikeable'?

_____

_____

_____

Person B is in the same situation and starts to think: 'Maybe something has held Matt up. He seems like a reliable person. It is unusual for him to be 30 minutes late for an appointment. Maybe he had a difficult customer, or the boss needed him. I will send a text later to see if everything is okay.'

How is person B feeling?

_____

_____

_____

Why do you think he or she feels this way?

_____

_____

_____

What is the difference between person B's thinking style compared to that of person A?

_____

_____

_____

Do you tend to think like person A? If so, in what ways?

_____

_____

_____

How could you think more like person B?

_____

_____

_____

Describe a work or life situation that you have experienced over the last few weeks where your thinking may have been unhelpful and self-critical, like the thinking of person A.

Situation:

_____

_____

_____

_____

_____

_____

_____

My thinking about the situation:

_____

_____

_____

_____

_____

_____

_____

ACTIVITY 2: Challenging Your Thoughts

Ask yourself: What was the evidence to confirm the thoughts you just described?

_____

_____

_____

_____

What could be alternative objective, realistic or more positive thoughts in the situation you have just described?

Remember, there is often an objective and positive side that we can miss initially. We can think: 'I am not going to let this get me down, I will give myself permission and encouragement to open my mind to other ways of thinking about this.'

Your alternative objective and realistic thoughts:

_____

_____

_____

_____

Your more positive and/or optimistic thoughts:

_____

_____

_____

_____

ACTIVITY 3: Recognizing Unhelpful Thinking Patterns

The following is a list of the common thinking patterns, identified by Professor Aaron Beck, that are associated with experiencing strong emotions such as anxiety, anger, depression and high stress levels:

- **Black and white thinking:** You think things are always one way or the other, for example, 'I can *never* do anything right'; 'It will *never* work'; 'I will *always* be unemployed.'
- **Overgeneralization:** Just because one thing goes wrong, you think everything will go wrong, for example, 'I just made a mistake at work, I bet I lose my job.'
- **Magical thinking:** You think you will have a bad day or something bad will happen based on the occurrence of something else completely unrelated – a superstitious reaction, for example, 'I had difficulty putting my seatbelt on this morning; that means I am going to have a bad day and have difficulty with everything.'
- **Mental filter:** Focusing on one or two details, and missing the big picture, for example, when your line manager is happy with the work you have shown her for a project, and you get into an argument because she is not prioritizing one or two details. She seems happy to let them go, but for you, the project will not be finished properly until you have attended to them.
- **Disqualifying the positive:** If something good happens you dismiss it as being irrelevant or unique and never to be repeated, for example 'My boss didn't really mean it when he said I went well today; he was just being nice.'
- **Jumping to conclusions:** You decide that you know what someone is thinking or feeling and what will happen in the future, even though you can't read someone else's mind or read the future. This is:
  - Mind reading, for example, 'None of my work colleagues like me, I can just sense it.'
  - Fortune telling, for example, 'I will start this job but I know I am going to lose it.'

- **Magnification and minimization:** You magnify the problems so that is all you see, and you minimize the positive. This distortion is:
    - Catastrophizing, which can be a characteristic of autism.
- **Emotional reasoning:** You think because you feel it, it must be true.
- **'Should' statements:** Your thoughts reflect rigid rules about how you or others 'should' behave, such as 'I should have known better' or 'I should have read the signals.'
- **Labelling and mislabelling:** You rely on naming yourself, others or events, and therefore miss out on a deeper or more accurate understanding of yourself, others or events, for example, 'I am a loser,' 'I am a natural victim' or 'That was a disaster.'
- **Personalization:** You think, 'It was all my fault,' even when you did not have control of everything that happened.

In the table below, tick the thinking patterns that you identify in yourself as being common.

Do you recognize any of these patterns of thinking in yourself?	Tick which apply
Black and white thinking	
Overgeneralization	
Magical thinking	
Mental filter	
Disqualifying the positive	
Jumping to conclusions	
Magnification and minimization	
Emotional reasoning	
'Should' statements	
Labelling and mislabelling	
Personalization	

This is a time to share with your mentor a work or life situation that is currently causing a problem or caused a problem in the past. With your mentor, identify any thinking distortions or errors that contributed to the problem continuing and affecting your wellbeing, and try to determine some good challenges for these thinking distortions.

Key points from your discussion:

_____

_____

_____

_____

_____

_____

_____

_____

ACTIVITY 4: Challenging Thinking Distortions

Below we present again common unhelpful patterns of thinking, but this time with challenges that you can experiment with to become more realistic rather than emotional in your appraisal of situations. Please resist the urge to be hard on yourself when you notice that you use these thinking styles. *We all use them when we are tired, stressed and emotional.* Problems can occur when the patterns become habitual. We know that many adults on the autism spectrum tend to use **black and white thinking**, a **mental filter**, **disqualifying the positive** and **personalization** at higher rates than people who do not have autism. Habitually falling into these thinking patterns may cause increased problems at work.

Black and white thinking

Things are rarely black and white; can you see the shades of grey in the situation? Instead of 'always', insert the word 'sometimes'. Look for the exception in what you are thinking.

> *Example:* There is no point trying; I always fail.

> *Realistic thinking:* I can learn from my mistakes. I can ask for help. If I ask for help, people will think I am constructively trying to solve the problem and that I am a friendly and wise person. There are many ways to solve the problem. If I keep trying, it is likely I will soon succeed.

Overgeneralization

Get back to the specifics. Think only about this moment, this time, this situation.

> *Example:* Grace did not call back, even though she said she would. I will never be able to make a good friend.

> *Realistic thinking:* Grace may have forgotten that she said she would call as she is incredibly busy at the moment. The battery of her mobile phone may be dead. If Grace does not want to be friends, there are many other people in the world. I will find others who may become good friends.

Magical thinking

Remind yourself that the concepts you are linking are totally unrelated. Just because one thing happened does not mean another thing will happen. Check if you are creating faulty logic.

Example: If I arrange all the cutlery in the cutlery drawer perfectly, today will go well.

Realistic thinking: I enjoy arranging all the cutlery in the cutlery drawer. Today will go well if I stay focused on what is happening in the moment and try to keep a positive attitude. Arranging the cutlery could not influence the actual events that I experience, but could affect how I perceive the events of the day.

Mental filter

Are you looking at the total situation, or focusing on just a few details? Those who have autism tend to over-focus on details, and especially errors. Mentally, take at least one step back and rethink the situation. Try to see what you are missing and the 'big picture', the overall effect. Ask someone else for their perspective if you cannot see it. There is always more information out there, and always many more perspectives than just one.

Example: Today everything I did made the situation worse.

Realistic thinking: Today I did some things well and I made some mistakes. This is because I am human. Making mistakes is helpful because I can learn from what happened. I will discuss what happened with my mentor and take advantage of the learning available in what happened today. I am happy with a lot of what I did today. The mistakes were only one part of the day.

Disqualifying the positive

The good things that are happening are just as relevant and important as the bad things that are happening. Start to trust that good things will happen to you, as well as bad things.

Examples: Only bad things ever happen to me. When people say something nice to me, they do it out of pity. The best event of my day happened because of luck, so it doesn't mean anything.

Realistic thinking: Both good and bad things happen to me. I will try to notice when good things are happening. I will amplify and accept these things into my life. I will get events into perspective and in balance.

Jumping to conclusions

No one knows the future. We cannot read minds. Start to accept that there will be uncertainty in life, and you will not always know what will lie ahead. This can be a good thing.

Example: This friendship will end badly; they always do.

Realistic thinking: I cannot predict the future. If I stay present to what is happening and keep a positive attitude, I can increase the chance of things working out well in this friendship, and I can learn from this experience to help with future friendships and relationships.

Magnification and minimization

Figuratively speaking, take out the mirror, not the magnifying glass or reversing the telescope. Look at the situation, or yourself, realistically rather than focusing only on what is wrong.

Example: I am a failure.

Realistic thinking: I made a mistake today, but I can learn from my mistake and next time I may be able to achieve success. Learning from mistakes makes me smarter and wiser.

Emotional reasoning

Feeling or thinking that something is true does not automatically make it true.

Example: I will always feel sad.

Realistic thinking: Just because I feel strongly that I will always feel sad does not mean it is true. I can take steps, like the ones in this programme, to overcome my sadness and start to feel pleasure and happiness again and enjoy being me.

'Should' statements

This means having high personal expectations and seeking perfection.

Example: I should be perfect, and I should never make a mistake at work.

Realistic thinking: No one is perfect, and everyone makes mistakes. I don't like making mistakes, but they are inevitable. I will try to stay calm so that I can stay smart and learn from this mistake.

Labelling and mislabelling

No person or situation can be solely defined by one label. Practising this way of thinking will seriously limit your understanding of a situation and your ability to be flexible in your perception and response.

Example: I am stupid.

Realistic thinking: Stupid is a negative label that will just make me feel bad. We can all do and say things that sometimes seem stupid, but this does not mean that we *are* stupid.

Personalization

Take a step back and view the situation objectively. Consider which parts of the situation you had control of or were responsible for, and which parts you didn't. Remember that you can never control someone else's behaviour or reaction to you, but you can control your own reaction.

Example: I did not get that job because I am a failure.

Realistic thinking: I don't know why I didn't get that job. There could be several reasons. Maybe there were a lot of applicants, and the best applicant had more experience than I have. Maybe I didn't come across well for the job interview. I can learn some skills to prepare well for future job interviews, to potentially make it a success next time. I will not let this get me down.

Discuss with your mentor realistic thoughts that would reduce any tendency that you may have for thinking distortions.

Key points from the discussion:

_____

_____

_____

_____

_____

_____

ACTIVITY 5: Consider Other Thinking Tools

From our extensive experience of supporting autistic adults, we recommend other Thinking Tools to help you in the workplace. These include:

- Giving yourself a **compliment** about your work abilities. This may change a negative and critical self-perception.
- Imagine what your **hero**, such as Dr Who, would do in that situation; for example, be brave and calm, and use Dr Who's intellect to find a solution.
- Create a **pleasures diary** that records in text and photographs any pleasures that you experience, from events and achievements to family members and pets. You could have the pleasures diary on your mobile phone and look at it as an antidote to poisonous thoughts.

Discuss how you could implement Thinking Tools at work and when you get home to create more realistic and optimistic thoughts and enhance your work performance and enjoyment of work.

Key points from the discussion:

_____

_____

_____

_____

_____

_____

_____

_____

_____

_____

Recommended further reading for Stage 5

Clark, D.A. and Beck, A.T. (2012) *The Anxiety and Worry Workbook: The Cognitive Behavioral Solution*. New York, NY: Guilford Press.

PERSONAL 'TAKE AWAYS' FROM STAGE 5

I recognize that I can tend to use the following unhelpful thinking patterns at times:

1. _____

2. _____

3. _____

4. _____

5. _____

Alternative, helpful thinking patterns I would like to use habitually are:

1. _____

2. _____

3. _____

4. _____

5. _____

My support team can help me in the following ways:

1. _____

2. _____

3. _____

4. _____

5. _____

Congratulations, you have now completed Stage 5!

Organizational Tools

▶ Thinking and learning abilities in autism

You can read the following information or watch the video recording '6.1 Thinking and learning abilities in autism'.

Adults who have autism have an unusual profile of cognitive (thinking and learning) abilities that can lead to talents that contribute to successful employment but also provide considerable stress in the workplace. The profile can include being talented in understanding the logical and physical world, noticing details and analysing and remembering and arranging information in a systematic fashion. However, there may be a propensity to be easily distracted, especially by detail, as well as being a perfectionist. When problem-solving, the person who has autism often appears to have a 'one-track mind', and thus experiences considerable difficulty 'changing track' while engaged in a 'train of thought'. There may also be problems with organizational abilities, such as determining what is going to be needed for a task, planning what to do and in the correct sequence, and time management, especially determining how long it will take to complete an activity. All these characteristics of cognitive abilities are described by psychologists as 'impaired executive function', and include:

- Organizational and planning abilities
- Working memory
- Inhibition and impulse control
- Self-reflection and self-monitoring
- Time management and prioritizing
- Incorporating new strategies
- Inhibiting an initial response.

Impaired executive function includes difficulties with inhibiting a response (being impulsive), working or short-term memory and using alternative strategies. An autistic person can be capable of thoughtful deliberation before responding, but under conditions of stress, especially when feeling overwhelmed or confused, they can be impulsive. It is important to relax and consider other options before responding and to recognize that being impulsive can be a sign of confusion and stress.

Working memory is the ability to hold information in mind when completing a task or solving a problem. An autistic person may have an exceptional long-term memory for facts and information but difficulty with the mental recall of recently presented information and manipulation of information relevant to a task. This is more apparent for auditory memory, such as recalling spoken instructions and conversation, but less for visual memory with the ability to easily create a mental photograph or video. An autistic person may have an auditory working memory capacity less than that of their work colleagues who have a 'bucket' capacity for remembering and using relevant spoken information; an autistic person has a memory 'cup' that affects the amount of information they can retrieve from their memory 'well'.

Another problem with working memory is a tendency to quickly forget a thought. One of the reasons those with autism are notorious for interrupting others was explained by someone with autism who said he had to say what was on his mind because if he waited, he would forget what he was going to say.

Another of the features of impaired executive function is difficulty in switching attention from one task to another. An autistic person usually has considerable problems switching thoughts to a new activity until there has been closure, that is, the current activity has been successfully completed. Those who do not have autism appear to be able to pause or close a thought or activity and to easily move to a different activity. In a work situation, an autistic person can find it difficult to switch activities before they have completed the previous activity, knowing that their thinking cannot cope as easily with transitions without closure. A line manager may need to provide multiple verbal warnings when an activity is going to change, potentially allowing the autistic person extra time to finish the task, as there can be a preference for quality over speed.

Impaired executive function can include a difficulty considering alternative problem-solving strategies, which could be represented by the metaphor of a train on a single track. If it is the right track, the person will quickly arrive at the destination, the solution to the problem. Unfortunately, those with autism can be the last to know if they are on the wrong track, or to recognize that there may be other tracks to the destination. Thus, there may be a problem with flexible thinking, one of the characteristics of impaired executive function. Neurotypical adults can quickly react to feedback and are prepared to change strategies or direction. Their vehicle of thought is not a train but a four-wheel drive vehicle that easily changes direction and is able to go 'off road'.

There can also be problems with self-reflection and self-monitoring. Neurotypical adults have the capacity to have a mental 'conversation' to solve a problem. The internal thinking process can include a dialogue or conversation, discussing the merits of various options and solutions. This process may not be as efficient in the thinking of an autistic person. Many autistic people 'think in pictures' and are less likely to use an inner voice or conversation to facilitate problem-solving.

An autistic person may prefer to use their own idiosyncratic approach to problem-solving, which we describe as the 'Frank Sinatra syndrome' or 'My Way'. Autistic adults may be famous (or even notorious) for being iconoclasts and rejecting popular beliefs and conventional wisdom. They do not consider the recommendations of their line manager, company procedures or the approaches being used by colleagues. This can have the potential advantage of producing an original response, not considered by other employees, but unfortunately the 'My Way' approach may lead to the line manager becoming exasperated trying to encourage the person to use conventional procedures or strategies. In addition, creative adults with autism, such as composers, engineers and architects, often cannot cope with any deviation from their original design. There can also be a fear of making a mistake – the emotional response to a mistake can be intense and inhibit perseverance.

We know that autistic adults tend to focus on the details of a problem. A detailed focus may identify aspects overlooked by others, a valued talent, but presents the disadvantage of responding emotionally to relatively less significant problems. Autistic people are often perfectionists with high, self-imposed standards of achievement, and tend to quickly abandon a project if there is little initial success.

It is also important to stay on top of paperwork and report writing and to meet anticipated deadlines.

However, we now recognize that significant advances in industry, science and the arts have been attributable to individuals who had a different way of thinking and possessed many of the cognitive characteristics associated with autism. Neurotypical people have a social or linguistic way of thinking, but there can be advantages in having an alternative perception and profile of cognitive abilities that can lead to valued talents. An autistic woman with considerable intellectual ability once said to Tony that 'language is a cage for thought'; many advances in science and the arts have been achieved by alternative conceptualizations that have not been based on linguistic thought.

ACTIVITY 1: Complete the Thinking and Learning Talents Questionnaire

Adults who have autism have an unusual profile of cognitive (thinking and learning) abilities that can lead to considerable success in the workplace. The autism cognitive profile can include being talented in some abilities, such as an expertise in remembering facts and information and originality in design and problem-solving.

This questionnaire is aimed at discovering abilities in your profile of cognitive abilities or talents.

6.1 Thinking and Learning Talents

Complete the following table.

Personal strengths in your cognitive abilities	Tick which apply
Long-term memory for facts and information	
Being an expert in an area of special interest	
Originality in problem-solving	
Being inventive	
Thinking in pictures	
Visual memory	
Being a craftsperson in areas such as woodwork	
Repairing things	
A particular sport, such as:	
Playing computer games, such as:	
A talent in the arts, such as:	
Playing an instrument	
Singing	
Drawing	
Animation	
Creative writing	

cont.

Personal strengths in your cognitive abilities	Tick which apply
Photography	
Being direct and to straight to the point	
Having a single-track focus	
Attention to detail	
Persistent	
Great at spotting patterns and errors	
Determined	
A fascination with symmetry and order	
High level of intellectual capacity	
High tolerance of repetitive tasks	
Pattern recognition	
Logic and analytic skills	
Attendance and punctuality	
Any other areas of talents and abilities?	

ACTIVITY 2: Identifying Useful Cognitive Strengths

Identify and discuss your cognitive talents and how these could be useful within a work situation.

Make notes during the discussion about how your cognitive strengths will be useful to you at work.

Are there any strengths that are currently not recognized at work that could be of benefit to your employer?

My personal talents are:	How this talent could be useful at work:

ACTIVITY 3: Complete the Cognitive or Organizational Difficulties Questionnaire

6.2 Cognitive or Organizational Difficulties

What are your difficulties with cognitive abilities such as organizing yourself, your environment and your time? Which of the following could give you problems in the workplace?

In the table, insert the degree of difficulty associated with each skill from 0 to 10, with 10 being *extremely difficult*.

Degree of difficulty	Rate 0–10
Knowing and organizing what will be needed for the task	
Planning your tasks over a day, a week and a month	
Working verbal memory (being able to remember something from several seconds to minutes whilst you think about or are distracted by something else)	
Estimating how long tasks will take	
Being distracted by details	
Remembering spoken instructions	
Inhibiting impulsive reactions or solutions	
Switching attention from one task to another	
Coping with mistakes	
Knowing if you are doing a good job	
Thinking of an alternative strategy	
Having higher standards than required	
Completing the activity in the correct sequence	
Complying with the conventional procedures	
Managing the urge to switch to a new activity before the current activity is completed	
Being able to inhibit impulsive responses	

Self-reflection and self-monitoring (internal conversation)	
Time management and prioritizing	
Managing procrastination (doing anything but the task at hand)	
Using new strategies	
Multiple focus or multi-tracking	
Prioritizing tasks when there are multiple requests	
Do you experience other cognitive or organizational difficulties that are not listed? What are they?	

Identify three cognitive or organizing abilities that you have most difficulty with and write them down here:

1. _____

2. _____

3. _____

Explore with your mentor in greater depth all the cognitive or organizational difficulties that you have identified, and the three with which you have the greatest difficulty.

How does each of these three difficulties affect you at work? How does it affect your work?

_____

_____

_____

_____

ACTIVITY 4: Strategies for Organizational Difficulties

▶ You can watch the video recording '6.2 Strategies for organizational difficulties'.

Discuss with your mentor strategies for managing difficulties with organizational abilities. Consider both personal coping methods and environmental modifications. We will now explore a range of tools for organizational difficulties.

Knowing and organizing what will be needed for the task

- Make a list in your notebook of what you need and cross off those items you have available with you before you commence the activity.
- Take a photograph with your mobile phone of the equipment or resources needed.

Additional strategies from the discussion:

_____

_____

Planning your tasks over a day, a week and a month

- Have a paper diary or electronic schedule app on your mobile phone, and create a schedule of activities.
- Estimate the amount of time needed for each activity and create a time schedule.

Additional strategies from the discussion:

_____

_____

Working verbal memory (being able to remember spoken instructions)

- Have your notebook with you and quickly write down or draw what you need to remember.
- Record the instructions on the audio-recording app on your mobile phone.
- As you listen to the instructions, create in your mind a video of what to do. You may be more able to remember the video than the spoken instructions.

Additional strategies from the discussion:

_____

_____

Estimating how long tasks will take

- Ask someone who has done the task before, a colleague or the person who gave you the instruction or request, how long it will probably take to complete the activity.
- Alternatively, make note of each stage of the task and estimate how long it will take to complete each, and then add up the times to estimate how long it will take to complete the whole task.

Additional strategies from the discussion:

_____

_____

Not being distracted by details

- Use an app on your mobile phone to make intermittent sounds that remind you to refocus on attending to the priority of completing the activity on time.

Additional strategies from the discussion:

_____

_____

Inhibiting impulsive reactions or solutions

- Think before you act. Be prepared to think of several responses before you act and decide which is the wisest response.

Additional strategies from the discussion:

_____

_____

Switching attention from one task to another

- Create an inner voice of a good friend, colleague or parent that reminds you to switch attention when needed. The 'voice' may say 'You need to stop and focus on the new activity.'
- You could also use an app on your mobile phone to make intermittent sounds to remind you to check if you should have switched attention.

Additional strategies from the discussion:

_____

_____

Coping with mistakes

- First, do not become distressed. Be calm and thoughtful. Mistakes happen and do not mean you are stupid or incompetent.
- Second, try to rectify the mistake; perhaps ask for help and guidance, which is the smart thing to do.

Additional strategies from the discussion:

_____

_____

Knowing if you are doing a good job

- Seek affirmation from your line manager or a colleague, but choose a time when the person is able to review and comment on your work and is not busy with another activity.

Additional strategies from the discussion:

_____

_____

Thinking of an alternative strategy

- The calmer you are, the more flexible and creative is your thinking, so that you can discover an alternative strategy.
- Consider asking someone to help, so that there are two minds working on finding a strategy.

Additional strategies from the discussion:

_____

_____

Having higher standards than required

- If your line manager is pleased with your work, that is enough.

Additional strategies from the discussion:

_____

_____

Completing the activity in the correct sequence

- Have a video or audio recording of the sequence of activities and make a note on your notepad of each component, in sequence. Then cross off each component when completed.

Additional strategies from the discussion:

_____

_____

Complying with the conventional procedures

- Learn the procedures, and have a copy that you can refer to, so that you can ensure that you have complied with your employer's expected procedures.

Additional strategies from the discussion:

_____

_____

Managing the urge to switch to a new activity before the current activity is completed

- Use the metaphor of a train arriving at a station. The train driver must wait for all the passengers to get off and on the train before starting the journey to the next station.

Additional strategies from the discussion:

_____

_____

Self-reflection and self-monitoring

- Try to develop the ability to silently talk to yourself about the activity as you are completing it. Your inner voice will be like a sports commentator on the radio explaining the sports event to the listeners. This will also facilitate concentration and inhibit distraction.

Additional strategies from the discussion:

_____

_____

Time management and prioritizing

- Make a list of the order of priorities and the amount of time needed for each activity. Use the stopwatch and alarm facility on your mobile phone to remind you when to focus on the next priority.

Additional strategies from the discussion:

_____

_____

Managing procrastination

- If you are 'frozen' in uncertainty or overwhelmed by complexity, practise a mindfulness activity, for example, the 3-minute activity of bringing each of the five senses into your mind, and sensing the information available to that sense.
- Decide to start on one task and give that task your full attention, as much as is possible to do so.
- Write down each task. Next, order them in terms of logic or priority, then choose one task to start. Commit to only one task at a time.
- Remember, you can only do one thing at a time, and just starting the task is the goal, not completing, and not doing a perfect job.

Additional strategies from the discussion:

_____

_____

Using new strategies

- Use a relaxation strategy, for example, five slow breaths, to calm your body down before trying a new strategy.
- Remind yourself that the new strategy may be better and is worth a try.

Additional strategies from the discussion:

_____

_____

Multiple focus or multi-tracking

- Use the relaxation strategies above to maximize the possibility of being as clear and calm as possible. If multi-tasking is still not possible, use Social Tools to develop a script to explain the issue to your line manager, to find a way around. It may be that you are better suited to tasks that require a single-minded focus.

Additional strategies from the discussion:

_____

_____

Prioritizing tasks when there are multiple requests

- Stop and use a relaxation strategy. Then ask yourself, 'What do I need to achieve first?' Or ask your line manager or a colleague for guidance on focus and priorities.

Additional strategies from the discussion:

_____

_____

Recommended further reading for Stage 6

Barkley, R. and Benton, C. (2010) *Taking Charge of Adult ADHD*. New York, NY: Guilford Press.

Boissiere, P. (2018) *Thriving with Adult ADHD: Skills to Strengthen Executive Functioning*. Emeryville, CA: Althea Press.

Ratey, J. and Hallowell, E. (2011) *Driven to Distraction: Recognizing and Coping with Attention Deficit Disorder*. New York, NY: Anchor Books.

Safren, S.A., Sprich, S.E., Perlman, C.A. and Otto, M.W. (2017) *Mastering Your Adult ADHD: A Cognitive-Behavioural Treatment Programme* (Second edition). Oxford: Oxford Clinical Psychology.

PERSONAL 'TAKE AWAYS' FROM STAGE 6

Three thinking and learning talents that I bring to work are:

1. _____

2. _____

3. _____

I sometimes experience these three difficulties with organizational skills:

1. _____

2. _____

3. _____

Three new ideas I could try to cope with the difficulties are:

1. _____

2. _____

3. _____

Three ways my support team could assist me are:

1. _____

2. _____

3. _____

Congratulations, you have now completed Stage 6!

Creation of a Personal Employment Plan

Purpose of the Personal Employment Plan

The Personal Employment Plan is essentially to assist you to communicate with your support team at work, especially your employer, the specific ideas and strategies that will assist you to succeed at work. During this programme we have covered many topics that are important to support you within your working life. Some of this information is personal and you would not feel comfortable, and it may not be appropriate, to share this information with people at work, for example, your manager. However, it will be helpful to share some of the information. Having autism and working with neurotypical colleagues can be a clash of cultures. People who are not on the autism spectrum often do not 'get' people who are, and autistic people often do not understand neurotypical colleagues either. What is needed is a 'cultural exchange' programme.

The Personal Employment Plan is structured to allow you to share information about autism and how this information applies to you. Within this stage we give you the opportunity to individualize the content, allowing you to convey to your employer and support team the tools, ideas and strategies that are likely to assist you to meet your goals, for example, to keep well organized and to manage social communication at work. The following pages are also available to download from https://library.jkp.com/redeem using the voucher code MMWZXGG.

ACTIVITY 1: Completing the Personal Employment Plan

The purpose of this plan is to create a booklet to share with your employer and/or colleagues a little about your personal strengths and competencies that can be of value in the workplace, and ideas and strategies to overcome specific challenges.

Discuss with your mentor the information you would like your employer to know. You may have concerns about how some of the information may be viewed or used. Now is a good time to voice those concerns with your mentor, and to also consider the potential advantages of sharing certain information.

With your mentor, complete the following sections based on the activities that you have completed in previous stages of the *Autism Working* programme.

My key overall strengths within the workplace (Stage 1):

_____

_____

_____

_____

_____

My key personality strengths within the workplace (Stage 3):

_____

_____

_____

_____

_____

My key cognitive talents within the workplace (Stage 6):

_____

_____

_____

_____

_____

Possible sources of work stress (Stage 1):

_____

_____

_____

_____

_____

_____

_____

_____

Factors that may increase work stress (Stage 1):

_____

_____

_____

_____

_____

_____

_____

My best strategies for work stress (Stage 1):

_____

_____

_____

_____

_____

_____

_____

_____

_____

_____

_____

_____

_____

_____

_____

_____

_____

_____

_____

_____

_____

_____

_____

_____

_____

Sensory issues at work (Stage 2):

_____

_____

_____

_____

_____

_____

_____

_____

_____

_____

Strategies and accommodations that help with sensory issues (Stage 2):

_____

_____

_____

_____

_____

_____

_____

_____

_____

_____

Specific social communication issues I may face in the workplace include (Stage 3):

_____

_____

_____

_____

_____

_____

_____

_____

_____

_____

_____

_____

Strategies my support team can use to help me with social communication difficulties (Stage 3):

_____

_____

_____

_____

_____

_____

_____

_____

_____

_____

Personal strategies for social communication issues I can use at work (Stage 3):

_____

_____

_____

_____

_____

_____

_____

_____

_____

_____

_____

_____

_____

_____

_____

_____

_____

_____

_____

_____

_____

Specific unhelpful thinking patterns I may use in the workplace include (Stage 5):

_____

_____

_____

_____

_____

_____

_____

_____

_____

_____

_____

_____

My support team can help me maintain realistic and helpful thinking by (Stage 5):

_____

_____

_____

_____

_____

_____

_____

_____

_____

Organizational difficulties I may experience at work (Stage 6):

_____

_____

_____

_____

_____

_____

_____

_____

My personal strategies for organizational difficulties include (Stage 6):

_____

_____

_____

_____

_____

_____

_____

_____

_____

Ways my support team can help with organizational difficulties I experience (Stage 6):

_____

_____

_____

_____

_____

_____

_____

_____

_____

Recommended further reading for Stage 7

Bissonnette, B. (2013) *Asperger's Syndrome Workplace Survival Guide: A Neurotypical's Secrets for Success*. London and Philadelphia, PA: Jessica Kingsley Publishers.

Edmonds, G. and Beardon, L. (2008) *Asperger Syndrome and Employment: Adults Speak Out about Asperger Syndrome*. London and Philadelphia, PA: Jessica Kingsley Publishers.

Simone, R. (2010) *ASD on the Job: Must-Have Advice for People with ASD or High Functioning Autism and their Employers, Educators, and Advocates*. Arlington, TX: Future Horizons.

Final words

Congratulations! You have now completed the *Autism Working* programme. Take some time to celebrate in a way that is meaningful to you. Your efforts are to be commended. The programme is effortful, but the work you have put in is worth it for the increased knowledge you have now gained to increase your self-awareness and skills to put into place in your workplace. Your Personal Employment Plan will arm you with the skills to manage a significant proportion of the difficulties that can arise in a workplace for autistic people, including difficulties with anxiety, worry and stress, sensory overload, unhelpful thinking patterns, difficulties with social communication, as well as organization and planning problems.

Have a copy of your Personal Employment Plan with you at work to refer to whenever you encounter difficulties at work due to having autism.

It may be helpful for you to share your Personal Employment Plan with your employer or HR staff support person. This is entirely your choice, but before deciding, speak with your mentor about the advantages and disadvantages of disclosure or not disclosing.

There are many excellent books and resources about autism and employment, and we have included a compendium of the best available to our knowledge at the time of going to print. This list is shared in Appendix D.

We would like to take this opportunity to wish you well for your employment goals, and to encourage you to put into place what you have learned during the course.

References

Attwood, T., Evans, C. and Lesko, A. (2014) *Been There. Done That. Try This! An Aspie's Guide to Life on Earth*. London and Philadelphia, PA: Jessica Kingsley Publishers.

Beck, A.T. (1975) *Cognitive Therapy and the Emotional Disorders*. Madison, CT: International Universities Press.

Ecker, C., Bookheimer, S. and Murphy, D. (2015) 'Neuroimaging in autism spectrum disorder: Brain structure and function across the lifespan.' *The Lancet/Neurology 14*, 1121–1134.

Fox, K.C.R., Nijeboer, S., Dixon, M.L., Floman, J.L. *et al.* (2014) 'Is meditation associated with altered brain structure? A systematic review and meta-analysis of morphometric neuroimaging in meditation practitioners.' *Neuroscience and Biobehavioural Reviews 43*, 48–73.

Griffiths, S., Allison, C., Kenny, R., Holt, R., Smith, P. and Baron-Cohen, S. (2019) 'The Vulnerability Experiences Quotient (VEQ): A study of vulnerability, mental health and life satisfaction in autistic adults.' *Autism Research 12*, 10.

Loundes-Taylor, J., Henninger, N.A. and Mailick, M.R. (2015) 'Longitudinal patterns of employment and postsecondary education for adults with autism and average-range IQ.' *Autism 19*, 7, 785–793.

Lovibond, S.H. and Lovibond, P.F. (1995) *Manual for the Depression Anxiety Stress Scales.* (2nd edn). Sydney, NSW: Psychology Foundation.

Manocha, R. (2016) *Silence Your Mind*. Sydney, NSW: Hachette.

Neary, P., Gilmore, L. and Ashburner, J. (2015) 'Post-school needs of young people with high-functioning Autism Spectrum Disorder.' *Research in Autism Spectrum Disorders 18*, 1–11.

Tavassoli, T., Hoekstra, R.A. and Baron-Cohen, S. (2014) 'The Sensory Perception Quotient (SPQ): Development and validation of a new sensory questionnaire for adults with and without autism.' *Molecular Autism 5*, 29.

Progressive Muscle Relaxation Script

Take some time now to settle yourself into a comfortable position. You may choose to sit in a comfortable armchair, or to lie down on the floor, on a mat, or on your bed. Make sure that you are warm. The body will cool down during this relaxation, but it is important that you remain comfortable. If you choose to lie down, please ensure that you place a pillow underneath your head to support your neck and head. Also ensure that your lower back is comfortable. Sometimes people find that it helpful to place a second pillow under the knees to take the pressure from the lower back.

Take these next few moments to check into your body to see if there are any other minor adjustments that you can make to make your body even 10 per cent more comfortable.

Consciously take in a deep breath through the nose, filling the lungs with oxygen, holding the breath for 3 seconds, and then gently and slowly release the breath through the nose. Take in another deep breath through the nose, hold your breath for 2 seconds, and then gently release the breath through the nose.

We are now going to start a wonderful relaxation strategy to bring calm and a sense of ease to the body. Thank yourself for giving yourself this time to practise relaxation, knowing that in the next few minutes there is nothing that you need to do, no one you need to see; this is a time just for you, to practise relaxation.

In progressive muscle relaxation (PMR), we mindfully bring tension into one part of the body only, and then mindfully release the tension from that part of the body. We do this in timing with our breath. Concentrate on taking a breath in whilst you bring tension into the part of the body being targeted.

On the release of tension, concentrate on releasing the breath at the same time. Whilst holding tension in one part of the body as requested, focus on relaxing the other parts of the body at the same time.

Hands

First, bring your attention to your hands. On the in-breath squeeze your hands into fists. Bring the tension into your body. Now hold the tension in your hands while you hold the breath for 3 seconds more. 1, 2, 3. Now release the breath and the tension at the same time, whilst counting to 3: 1, 2, 3. Feel the tension leave your hands. Feel softness where there was tension. Wonderful, well done.

Arms

I want you now to bring your attention to your arms. Whilst taking in a breath and counting to 3, hold your arms out in front of you, bringing tension into the arms to make both the forearms and the upper arms stiff like a board. Hold the tension for a count of 3. 1...hold the tension, 2...squeeze, 3...release the tension from the arms and release the breath at the same time whilst counting to 3: 1, 2, 3. Feel softness in the arms where before they were tense and stiff. Allow softness and stillness to be in the arms now.

Shoulders and neck

Now, whilst relaxing the rest of your body, bring your attention to your shoulders and neck. Whilst taking in a breath and counting to 3, squeeze your shoulders toward your ears, bringing tension into the neck to the level that is comfortable for you. Hold and squeeze for 3. 1...squeeze, 2...hold, 3...release the tension and the breath at the same time whilst counting to 3: 1, 2, 3. Well done. Welcome the ease and softness into your shoulders and neck.

Face

Now, whilst relaxing the rest of your body, bring your attention to your face. Take in a breath, screw your face up into a grimace, bringing tension into all the small muscles of your face including your tongue and jaw. Hold for 3. 1...squeeze, 2...hold, 3...release the tension and the breath at the same time whilst counting to 3: 1, 2, 3. Feel the jaw and facial muscles soften and relax. Wonderful work.

Stomach

Moving down the body, bring your attention to your stomach. We tend to hold a lot of tension in our stomachs. If you know this is true for you, I recommend that you gently place loving hands on your stomach for this part of the exercise. This will allow you to release even more tension. Whilst taking in a breath and counting to 3, contract your stomach muscles together, drawing your energy in as if you were about to lift your legs off the floor using only your stomach muscles. Hold the tension to a level that is comfortable for you. Hold and squeeze for a count of 3. 1...squeeze, 2...hold, 3...gently release the tension in your stomach and release the breath at the same time whilst counting to 3: 1, 2, 3. Well done. If you have your hands on your stomach, you may now gently move them to the floor or the arms of the chair. Relax the whole of your body; let go of all tension.

Buttocks

Now, bring your attention to your buttocks. Whilst taking in a breath and counting to 3, squeeze the cheeks of your buttocks together, bringing tension to the them. Hold for 3. 1...squeeze your buttocks, 2...hold the tension, 3... release the tension and the breath at the same time whilst counting to 3: 1, 2, 3. Good.

Legs

Now, whilst relaxing the rest of your body, bring your attention to your legs, the whole length of the legs at once. Whilst taking in a breath and counting to 3, bring tension into the whole of your legs. To do so, focus on tensing up the calf and the thigh muscles in both legs at the same time. Hold for a count of 3. 1...hold the tension, 2...hold, 3...release the tension and the breath at the same time whilst counting to 3: 1, 2, 3. Good work. Notice the softness in the muscles of your legs as you let go of all the tension.

Feet

Take a moment to relax the whole of your body. Now bring your attention to your feet. Whilst taking in a breath and counting to 3, bring tension into your feet to a level that is comfortable for you. Squeezing the toes downward toward the heels can be one way of bringing tension into the feet. Squeeze and hold for 3 with the breath. 1...squeeze, 2...hold, 3...release the tension and the breath at the same time whilst counting to 3: 1, 2, 3. Relax the feet. Allow them to rest on the floor, or, if you are lying down, to flop to each side.

Whole body

Now, we are going to tense the whole body at once. Draw in the breath, and whilst counting to 3, bring tension into the whole of your body. Ball up your fists, straighten your arms and legs, screw your face up into a grimace, ball up your feet, squeeze your shoulders toward your ears, and squeeze your stomach and buttock muscles together. Squeeze and hold the tension for a count of 3. 1…squeeze all parts of your body, 2…hold, 3…release the tension and the breath at the same time whilst counting to 3: 1, 2, 3. Excellent work.

Now it is time to simply relax and let go of all the tension that has been brought into the body. Gently allow your awareness to touch on each part of the body as I name that part. As your awareness gently touches each part of the body, say in your own mind, 'relax, let go'. Hands…, arms…, shoulders…, neck…, face…and jaw…, stomach…, buttocks…, legs…, feet… The whole of your body, just relaxing. Give yourself permission to stay in this position for a few moments. This is relaxation. It is a different state to muscle tension. Relaxed muscles give a message to our brain to be calm. Remember this feeling of relaxation; it is yours whenever you need it. The more you practise relaxation, the more quickly, comfortably and easily you will be able to relax. Learning to relax is a skill that is worth learning. Remember, it is a practice, not a performance. The mind may judge what you are doing here. If you notice your mind is judging you or what you are doing, just notice and let that go. Bring your mind back the sensation of rest, softness, relaxation in the muscles. A relaxed body is a relaxed mind.

Now, gently begin to wiggle your fingers and toes. Gently move your head from side to side. Do what you need to do to bring energy back into your body: stretch, sigh, yawn. If you are lying down, roll your body to the side, allowing yourself to rest in a foetal position for a moment before gently sitting up. Gently open your eyes, and thank yourself for giving your mind and body this beautiful practice. Gently now move through the rest of the activities of your day, consciously allowing yourself to relax when tension starts to come back into the body. Have a beautiful, relaxed day.

Social Support Network

Personal support	• Family, friends • Psychologist, doctor • Social or interest group	
Workplace support	• HR manager • Supervisor or manager • Colleagues	
Individual plan	• Mentor to support management and review of plan • Personal Employment Plan	

Speaking Aspergerese

Aspergerese: A different culture and way of thinking

Aspergerese	Why	What to do
Not looking at me when I talk	Helps with processing what is said	Understand the person is still listening, don't take it personally
Pointing out my errors and criticizing me	Trying to be helpful, trying to increase own sense of value, too honest	Don't be offended, thank the person
Takes a long time to reply	Processes spoken language and social information more slowly	Be patient, allow time
Talks for a long time with a lot of detail	Values detail, knowledge and getting it right	Thank the person and ask for the short version
Extremely sensitive to implication of stupidity	Values intellect highly	Apologize and compliment the person's intellect

List of Helpful Resources

Book title	Author(s)	Publisher	Notes
An Asperger's Guide to Entrepreneurship: Setting Up Your Own Business for Professionals with Autism Spectrum Disorder	Rosalind A. Bergemann	Jessica Kingsley Publishers	Describes how to set up your own business
Asperger's Syndrome Workplace Survival Guide: A Neurotypical's Secrets for Success	Barbara Bissonnette	Jessica Kingsley Publishers	All three of Barbara's books are recommended
Helping Adults with Asperger's Syndrome Get & Stay Hired: Career Coaching Strategies for Professionals and Parents of Adults on the Autism Spectrum	Barbara Bissonnette	Jessica Kingsley Publishers	
The Complete Guide to Getting a Job for People with Asperger's Syndrome: Find the Right Career and Get Hired	Barbara Bissonnette	Jessica Kingsley Publishers	
Autism Equality in the Workplace: Removing Barriers and Challenging Discrimination	Janine Booth	Jessica Kingsley Publishers	Focus includes workplace discrimination and workplace adjustments
Unemployed on the Autism Spectrum: How to Cope Productively with the Effects of Unemployment and Job Hunt with Confidence	Michael John Carley	Jessica Kingsley Publishers	Useful for those seeking employment

Asperger Syndrome & Employment: Adults Speak Out about Asperger Syndrome	Edited by Genevieve Edmonds and Luke Beardon	Jessica Kingsley Publishers	Wise overall advice
Employment for Individuals with Asperger Syndrome or Non-Verbal Learning Disability	Yvona Fast and others	Jessica Kingsley Publishers	Good information on reading body language, conversation skills and coping with bullying
Developing Talents: Careers for Individuals with Asperger Syndrome and High-Functioning Autism	Temple Grandin and Kate Duffy	Autism Asperger Publishing Company	Recommended reading for sensory sensitivity and strategies, and the value of a mentor
How to Find Work That Works for People with Asperger Syndrome: The Ultimate Guide for Getting People with Asperger Syndrome into the Workplace (and keeping them there!)	Gail Hawkins	Jessica Kingsley Publishers	Useful for those seeking employment
Auti Power! Successful Living and Working with an Autism Spectrum Disorder	Herman Jansen and Betty Rombout	Jessica Kingsley Publishers	Useful information
Managing with Asperger Syndrome	Malcolm Johnson	Jessica Kingsley Publishers	Valuable strategies when promoted to management
Asperger Syndrome Employment Workbook: An Employment Workbook for Adults with Asperger Syndrome	Roger N. Meyer	Jessica Kingsley Publishers	The first and still one of the best books on employment
The Wonderful World of Work: A Workbook for Asperteens	Jeanette Purkis	Jessica Kingsley Publishers	A workbook for teenagers transitioning between education and employment

cont.

Book title	Author(s)	Publisher	Notes
Developing Workplace Skills for Young Adults with Autism Spectrum Disorder: The BASICS College Curriculum	Michelle Rigler, Amy Rutherford and Emily Quinn	Jessica Kingsley Publishers	Information on the transition from education to employment
ASD on the Job: Must-Have Advice for People with ASD or High Functioning Autism and their Employers, Educators, and Advocates	Rudy Simone	Future Horizons, Inc.	Useful information
Business for Aspies	Ashley Stanford	Jessica Kingsley Publishers	The author is the CEO of a computer company in Silicon Valley
Employing People with Asperger Syndrome: A Practical Guide	Various	Prospects/ The National Autistic Society	Valuable information
Asperger Syndrome and Employment	Sarah Hendrickx	Jessica Kingsley Publishers	What works and doesn't work for work
The Neurodiverse Workplace: An Employer's Guide	Victoria Honeybourne	Jessica Kingsley Publishers	A resource for employers
An Employer's Guide to Managing Professionals on the Autism Spectrum	Marcia Scheinder and Joan Bogden	Jessica Kingsley Publishers	A guide for managers and colleagues

The Autism-Friendly Guide to Self-Employment

Robyn Steward

£12.99 | $17.95 | PB | 192PP | ISBN 978 1 78775 532 1 | eISBN 978 1 78775 533 8

This practical guide helps autistic people and those who support them explore self-employment so they can do what they are passionate about. It provides advice on being self-employed, including how to work out how much to charge, how to get paid, tips on networking, managing tax and other legal requirements. It also explains how to navigate welfare systems for support. This is the essential guide to discovering self-employment and being part of a local community.

Robyn Steward is an autistic woman with experience of mentoring others on the spectrum, and author of *The Independent Woman's Handbook for Super Safe Living on the Autistic Spectrum* (2013) and *The Autism-Friendly Guide to Periods* (2019). Robyn is successfully self-employed and is an NAS ambassador and regularly appears on TV and radio. She is also co-host of the BBC Sounds podcast *1800 Seconds on Autism*.

Mploy – A Job Readiness Workbook
Career Skills Development for Young Adults on the Autism Spectrum and with Learning Difficulties

Michael P. McManmon with Jennifer Kolarik and Michele Ramsay
Foreword by Carol Gray

£35 | $55 | PB | 192PP | ISBN 978 1 78592 730 0 | eISBN 978 1 78450 408 3

This ready-to-use workbook provides everything you need to help young people with autism or learning differences prepare for work. Suitable for those working with young adults aged 16–26, this workbook includes activities and worksheets designed to develop key skills for meaningful careers, so young people can enter employment with confidence.

Dr Michael P. McManmon is the founder of the College Internship Program (CIP), that prepares young adults with learning differences and on the autism spectrum with academic, career, social and independent living skills, at five centers across the USA.

Dr Michele Ramsay is a Program Director at CIP Brevard and has 18 years of experience in school district management.

Jennifer Kolarik is a Lead Career Coordinator at CIP and has over 20 years of experience working with teens and young adults.

Helping Adults with Asperger's Syndrome Get & Stay Hired

Career Coaching Strategies for Professionals and Parents of Adults on the Autism Spectrum

Barbara Bissonnette

£15.99 | $24.95 | PB | 224PP | ISBN 978 1 84905 754 7 | eISBN 978 1 78450 052 8

Written for professionals and parents, this book offers employment strategies to support individuals with Asperger's Syndrome (Autism Spectrum Disorder) into fulfilling and long-lasting careers. It provides a primer on how people with Asperger's Syndrome think and teaches coaching techniques to help with job hunting and workplace challenges.

Barbara Bissonnette is a certified coach and the principal of Forward Motion Coaching. She specializes in career development coaching for adults with Asperger's Syndrome and Non-Verbal Learning Disorder. Barbara is the author of *The Complete Guide to Getting a Job for People with Asperger's Syndrome* and *Asperger's Syndrome Workplace Survival Guide*. She lives in Stow, Massachusetts.

Autism Equality in the Workplace
Removing Barriers and Challenging Discrimination

Janine Booth
Foreword by John McDonnell MP

£12.99 | $19.95 | PB | 128PP | ISBN 978 1 84905 678 6 |
eISBN 978 1 78450 197 6

People with autism often find themselves excluded from working life. This practical handbook lays out reasonable, achievable ways in which working environments can be adapted and people with autism included as valuable members of the workforce.

Janine Booth is a workplace trade union representative and co-chair of the TUC Disabled Workers' Committee. She is autistic, and has an autistic son, and is a walking advertisement for autism in the workplace. Janine wrote the TUC Disabled Workers' Conference policy on Autism in the Workplace and runs training events for the Workers' Educational Association and for trade unions.

Launching Your Autistic Youth to Successful Adulthood

Everything You Need to Know About Promoting Independence and Planning for the Future

Katharina Manassis

£14.99 | $19.95 | PB | 240PP | ISBN 978 1 78775 345 7 | eISBN 978 1 78775 346 4

This book addresses the concerns parents of autistic teenagers may have as their child transitions to adult life. It explores specific aspects of adult life such as independence, employment and social life, and offers practical solutions for common transition-related challenges such as finding suitable living arrangements and financial planning.

Katharina Manassis is Professor Emerita at the University of Toronto. She is a retired child psychiatrist and mother to an autistic son who has successfully transitioned to adulthood. She lives in Ontario, Canada.

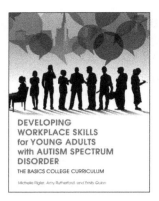

DEVELOPING
WORKPLACE SKILLS
for YOUNG ADULTS
with AUTISM SPECTRUM
DISORDER
THE BASICS COLLEGE CURRICULUM

Michelle Rigler, Amy Rutherford, and Emily Quinn

Developing Workplace Skills for Young Adults with Autism Spectrum Disorder

The BASICS College Curriculum

Michelle Rigler, Amy Rutherford and Emily Quinn

£24.99 | $39.95 | PB | 224PP | ISBN 978 1 84905 799 8 | eISBN 978 1 78450 097 9

This practical college curriculum helps students with Autism Spectrum Disorder (ASD) to enter into working life with confidence. With visual reinforcements and exercises, it teaches young people strategies for managing the stresses and challenges of employment.

Michelle Rigler, EdD, is Director of the Disability Resource Center at the University of Tennessee at Chattanooga and Director of the Mosaic Program for students with Autism Spectrum Disorder on which the BASICS Curriculum is based.

Amy Rutherford, MEd, is Assistant Director and an instructor for the Disability Resource Center's Mosaic Program for students with Autism Spectrum Disorder at the University of Tennessee at Chattanooga.

Emily Quinn, MEd, is Interim Assistant Director of the Disability Resource Center and serves in the role of coach and instructor for the Mosaic Program for Students with Autism Spectrum Disorder at the University of Tennessee at Chattanooga.